THE SANDWICH TOASTER COOKBOOK

THE SANDWICH TOASTER COOKBOOK

OMEGA BOOKS

This edition published 1983 by Omega Books Ltd,
1 West Street, Ware, Hertfordshire, under licence
from the proprietor.

Copyright © Paul Hamlyn Pty Ltd 1980

ISBN 0 907853 16 1

Printed and bound in Hong Kong by South China Printing Co.

Introduction

People who prepare and cook food everyday will find this book an interesting source of new recipes cooked in sandwich-toasting appliances. 'Snackmaking the easy way', will provide many suggestions to vary the daily menu and show you how to make better use of your appliance, whether you have a 4-Up or 8-Up Snackmaker, a Snack 'n' Sandwich Toaster or an Electric Jaffle.

With an emphasis on preparing and serving snacks, the book contains many ideas for sandwich fillings with a difference, plus a collection of recipes which will appeal to the younger members of the family since they were concocted by a group of children.

In addition the book includes recipes for starters, main courses and desserts with a special section on accompaniments. You will be surprised at the variety of different meals which may be made using the sandwich-toasting appliances. Fresh, canned or frozen 'convenience' foods are used in the ingredients and of course, these appliances provide the ideal way in which to use leftovers. The versatility of the appliances is well demonstrated in the section on hors d'oeuvre or starters — tasty delicacies to serve with drinks — with such recipes as Devils on Horseback, Spinach Oyster Tarts, Sausage Rolls and Red Riders. Pastries and doughs may be used in the appliances instead of breads so sections on quiches and pizzas have been included. Spring rolls are another unusual dish which may be cooked quickly in a Snackmaker, with very attractive and delicious results.

Create new dessert delights using leftover cake or Puff Pastry and a delicious filling. The book also contains recipes for old favourites such as Apple Charlotte and Orange Scones. Cook them in minutes in your Electric Jaffle or Snackmaker and since you won't need to turn on the oven you will be reducing the electricity bill. For a special treat make some individual Bombe Alaskas or crisp and golden French Waffles filled with strawberries, using another of the versatile appliances, the Wafflemaker. Suggested fillings for waffled sandwiches are also included.

So whether you are making a snack, hors d'oeuvre, a luncheon dish or dessert, you will find that the recipes contained in 'Snackmaking the easy way' are easy to prepare and the delicious results will be ready to serve in minutes. Your appliance will become an invaluable asset when preparing and cooking snacks and meals for the family or entertaining friends. 'Snackmaking the easy way' is a book which the whole family will appreciate and enjoy.

Contents

Consult the index on pages 102 and 103 where recipes have been cross-referenced according to their main ingredients. Main sections with their recipes are also listed.

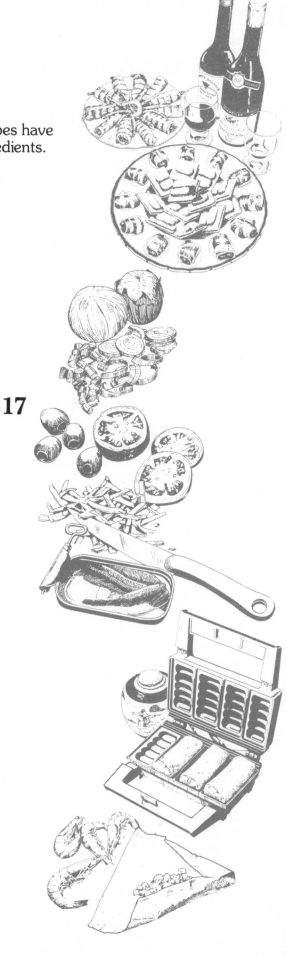

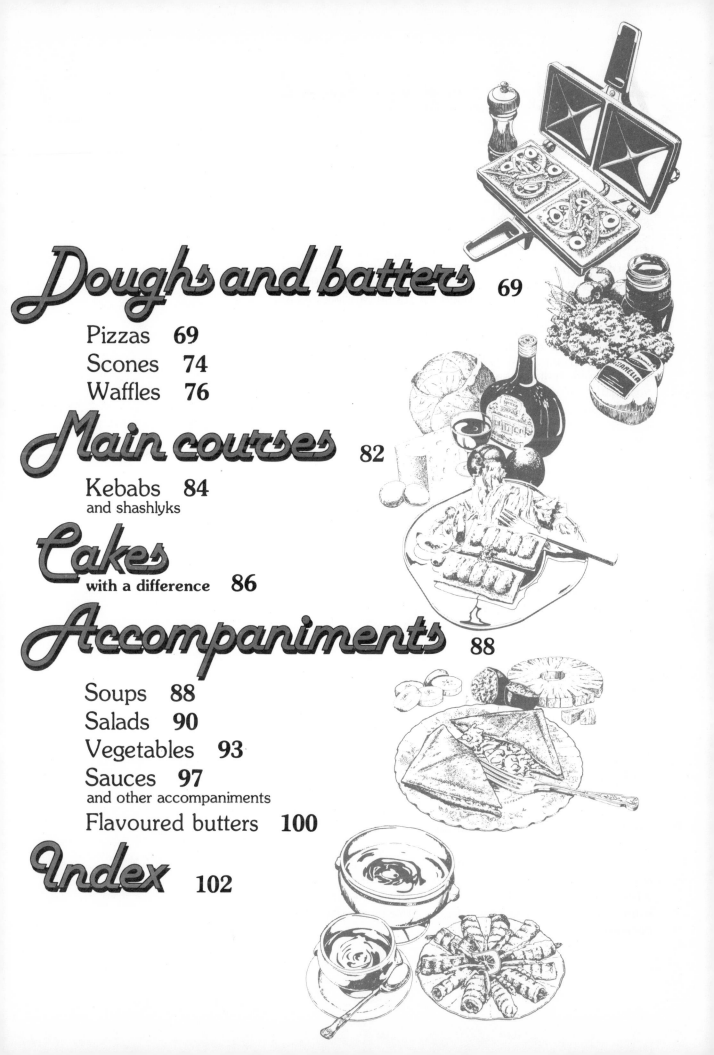

How to use this book

Appliances

For most recipes, a Snack 'n' Sandwich Toaster, a 4-Up or 8-Up Snackmaker or an Electric Jaffle may be used. In general the recipes refer to the appliance used as a Sandwich Toaster.
Where it is advisable to use a specific appliance or a recipe cannot be made using a particular one, this is stated in the method. A Wafflemaker is unsuitable for most of the recipes and should only be used for those sandwiches and waffles in that section.
Where a recipe requires 8 slices of bread to make 4 sandwiches, for example, and you are using a Snack 'n' Sandwich Toaster, 4-Up Snackmaker or Electric Jaffle, simply make half the sandwiches, keep them warm and repeat the procedure. Similarly if you have an 8-Up Snackmaker, ingredients may be doubled where recipes contain amounts for smaller appliances.

Serves

Each recipe states how many rolls, puffs and so on that the amount of ingredients will make. The figure will vary depending on how much filling is used for each item made. The amount will also vary with different appliances. The Electric Jaffle uses more filling than the Snackmakers and Snack 'n' Sandwich Toaster. In addition, if the rolls or puffs are served as hors d'oeuvre you will probably need less per person than if you intend to serve them as a luncheon dish or snack.

Breads

Size of bread slice, piece of pastry or dough used is important. For bread, use slices measuring approximately 11 cm square; sizes of pastry required for particular appliances are given on page 52. Thick toasting bread is recommended to ensure even browning of the sandwich. With thick bread, only a small amount of filling should be used, however when using sandwich bread, more filling will be required.
The best breads to use are brown or white milkbread, light rye, sourdough, raisin, Lebanese flatbread, kibbled wheat or grainy bread. Some of the protein-enriched breads and black bread tend to become hard when cooked.

Minis and Rolls

Mini sandwiches are fun to make and may be served on many occasions. Prepare the sandwiches using any of the fillings. Use the 4-Up or 8-Up Snackmaker or the Snack 'n' Sandwich Toaster then turn them halfway through the cooking time, across the cutters, thus dividing the sandwich into 4 sealed sections. This can also be done when making pies and puffs.
Attractive rolls may also be made in a Snackmaker by turning the rectangular-shaped sandwiches or puffs in the scallops during the cooking time. Examples of rolls and mini sandwiches are shown in the second colour photograph in this book.

Butters

For the sake of simplicity I have called the lubricant 'butter', but bacon or chicken fat, vegetable oil, margarine or non-stick cooking spray may be used on the appliance before preheating. The instructions 'butter the bread' or 'brush with melted butter' are interchangeable. Detailed instructions for the use of specific fats needed when cooking pastry, dough and batter are given at the beginning of the sections concerned.

Coatings

Added flavour may be achieved by using one of the Flavoured Butters, which begin on page 100. Dipping the bread into beer, sauces, fruit juice, chocolate and sugar also gives added interest to the taste.

Acknowledgements

Thank you to Breville who supplied the appliances and some of the recipes used in this book; and also John West for supplying food for testing the recipes.

A special thank you to Georgia, Anna, Emily, Judy, Renata, Frazer, Tim and Ashley.

Contributors

Where a name and address appears below a particular recipe, this indicates that the idea was originated by that person. Special thanks are extended to those people for their welcome contributions.

Weights and Measures

The metric weights and fluid measures refer to those of the Standards Association of Australia. A set of metric spoons and cups are very helpful and can be obtained readily from most hardware and department stores. The Australian Standard measuring cup has a capacity of 250 millilitres (250 ml). The Australian Standard measuring spoon has a capacity of 20 millilitres (20 ml). Cups and spoons are made in set of 4. All cup and spoon measurements are level and all flour is plain, unless otherwise stated. A good set of scales is an asset in any kitchen.

IMPORTANT POINTS
New Zealand, Canadian and American weights and measures are the same with the exception that the Australian standard measuring tablespoon is larger than that of New Zealand, Canada and America, having a capacity of 20 millilitres (20 ml) compared to 15 millilitres (15 ml) in New Zealand and North America. For accuracy use 4 teaspoonsful (or 4 x 5-millilitre measuring spoons) in New Zealand and North America when the recipe specifies 1 tablespoon. It is also important to note that the New Zealand and Australian imperial pint has a capacity of 20 fluid ounces whereas the North American pint has a capacity of 16 fluid ounces.

NOTE
For successful cooking use either one or other of the measuring systems — all metric or all imperial — do not use a mixture. The metric yield of cup or weighed measures is about 10 per cent greater than that of imperial but the proportions of either system are the same within each one.

VOLUME				WEIGHT	
METRIC		**IMPERIAL**		**METRIC**	**IMPERIAL**
millilitres	cups	fluid ounces		grams	ounces
30 ml		1 fl oz		15 g	½ oz
	¼ cup	2 fl oz		30 g	1 oz
100 ml		3 fl oz		60 g	2 oz
	½ cup	4 fl oz	(¼ pint US)	90 g	3 oz
150 ml		5 fl oz	(¼ pint imp)	125 g	4 oz (¼ lb)
	¾ cup	6 fl oz		185 g	6 oz
250 ml	1 cup	8 fl oz	(½ pint US)	250 g	8 oz (½ lb)
	1¼ cups	10 fl oz	(½ pint imp)	375 g	12 oz (¾ lb)
	1½ cups	12 fl oz		500 g (0.5 kg)	16 oz (1 lb)
	1¾ cups	14 fl oz		750 g	24 oz (1½ lb)
500 ml	2 cups	16 fl oz		1000 g (1 kg)	32 oz (2 lb)
	2½ cups	20 fl oz		1500 g (1.5 kg)	3 lb
1 litre	4 cups	32 fl oz		2000 g (2 kg)	4 lb

Starters

These are delicious bits and pieces that are nice to serve before dinner with the family or when friends visit. Starters should be simple to prepare and small enough to eat easily with the fingers. Ensure that fillings are not too runny. Prepare the ingredients in advance then use your Sandwich Toaster, Snackmaker or Electric Jaffle to cook them perfectly in minutes.

The flavour and quantity of starters served should be enough to whet the appetite and complement the flavour of the meal to come. Many of the fillings and ideas in this section can double for snacks or in some cases more substantial meals. Halfway through the cooking time turn the sandwich or filled pies around to make minis. The Electric Jaffle is ideal for Wrap Arounds and other tempting bits on sticks. Attractive hors d'oeuvre may be made by placing sandwiches in the Wafflemaker, to give them a crisp and unusual appearance. Try the suggestions here, but then experiment with your own favourite fillings as well.

Spinach Oyster Tarts

Serves 4-8

1 quantity Shortcrust Pastry (see
    page 53) or 1 packet frozen
    shortcrust pastry
melted butter for brushing
1 cup leftover cooked spinach
1 tablespoon cream
1 x 100-g can smoked oysters
60 g gruyère cheese, grated
cayenne pepper

This is a good way to use up any leftover spinach (silver beet) as very little is required.
Roll pastry to thickness of 3 mm and cut 8 pieces to fit scallops of Sandwich Toaster. Brush melted butter lightly on 1 side of each piece. Preheat Sandwich Toaster. Place spinach in bowl and beat with cream until well combined. Season if necessary with salt and pepper. Lay a piece of pastry in each scallop, buttered side down, divide spinach mixture between scallops and top with smoked oysters. Sprinkle with grated cheese, cover with remaining pastry, buttered sides up, and cook for 3-5 minutes until pastry is golden. Sprinkle tarts lightly with cayenne and serve hot.
Variation: Used either in pastry or bread this filling makes an excellent accompaniment to grilled ham steaks.

Cheese and Onion Puffs
(Pictured on page 19)
Serves 4-8

1 quantity Puff Pastry (see page 52)
or 1 packet frozen puff pastry
non-stick cooking spray or melted
butter
1 large onion, minced or very finely
sliced
200 g Cheddar cheese, grated
salt and pepper to taste
pinch nutmeg

Roll pastry to thickness of 3 mm. Cut into 8 pieces the size of the toaster scallops. Spray scallops with non-stick cooking spray or brush melted butter lightly on 1 side of each piece of pastry. Preheat Sandwich Toaster. Mix together the onion and grated cheese and season well with salt, pepper and nutmeg. Lay a piece of pastry in each scallop, buttered side down. Divide cheese mixture between them and cover with remaining pastry, buttered sides up. Cook for 4-5 minutes, turning halfway through cooking time to make small puffs. Serve hot.
Variation: Cheese, Apple and Onion Puffs. Add 1 Granny Smith apple, peeled, cored and finely chopped and reduce amount of cheese to 125 g. Proceed as above.

Sausage Rolls
(Pictured on page 19)
Serves 10-12

1 quantity Puff Pastry (see page 52)
or 1 packet frozen puff pastry
melted butter for brushing
125 g sausage meat
1 small onion, minced or very finely
chopped
¼-½ teaspoon mixed dried herbs
salt and pepper to taste

Roll pastry to a thickness of 3 mm and cut into rectangles 5 x 10 cm. Lightly brush 1 side of each rectangle with melted butter. Preheat Sandwich Toaster or Electric Jaffle. Mix sausage meat with minced onion and herbs. Season to taste with salt and pepper. Lay a small roll of sausage mixture along the centre of each piece of pastry and roll up. Lay rolls vertically in scallops or side by side in the Electric Jaffle. Use kitchen scissors to snip 3 or 4 cuts along the top of each roll before cooking, this gives an attractive appearance to the rolls. Close and cook for 5-6 minutes. Do not clamp.
Note: To make bite-sized sausage rolls cut the filled rolls in half, using kitchen scissors, before cooking.

Guacamole Delights

Serves 4-8

8 slices white milk bread
melted butter for brushing
2 ripe medium avocados
1 small onion, roughly chopped
1 tablespoon white vinegar
salt and freshly ground black
pepper to taste
1 green capsicum, roughly
chopped

Preheat Sandwich Toaster. Brush 1 side of each bread slice with melted butter. Either purée remaining ingredients in the Kitchen Wizz or blender or mash thoroughly together. Divide mixture between 4 bread slices, cover with remaining bread and cook for 2 minutes, turning sandwiches after 1 minute.
Note: Depending on the size of the avocados you may have sufficient filling for 10 slices of bread.
Variation: Guacamole Dip. The filling ingredients after puréeing also make a superb dip. Serve chilled with small crackers or chips.

Avocado Nibbles

Serves 4-8

8 slices Vogel's or milk bread
melted butter for brushing
1 large or 2 small ripe avocados,
   peeled and mashed
juice 1 large lemon
salt
freshly ground black pepper

Preheat Sandwich Toaster. Brush 1 side of each bread slice lightly with melted butter. Spread avocado over 4 slices of bread, unbuttered sides. Sprinkle with lemon juice and season generously with salt and lashings of freshly ground black pepper. Cover with remaining bread slices, buttered sides up. Cook for 2 minutes, turning the sandwiches halfway through the cooking time to make double cuts.

Croque Madame

Serves 4

8 slices white bread, with crusts
approximately 1 cup beer
butter
1 cup grated Parmesan cheese

This is a very special version of a Parisian hors d'oeuvre. Traditionally they are served small and the Snackmakers and Sandwich Toasters are perfect to cook them in.
Pour the beer into a shallow dish. Dip each side of the bread slices into the beer. Lay the dipped slices onto a paper-towel covered rack and leave the bread to dry. When the bread has dried, cut off the crusts and butter both sides of each slice.
Preheat Sandwich Toaster, lay bread slices into the scallops and divide the cheese between the 4 bases of the sandwiches. Top with remaining bread, close toaster and cook for 2 minutes or until crisp and golden. Serve hot.
Note: This is also very good cooked in the Wafflemaker.

Croque Monsieur

Serves 4-8

8 slices white bread
butter
1 x 60-g egg
125 ml milk
4 slices Swiss cheese
4 slices ham

This old-time favourite is very easy to make. Served whole Croque Monsieur makes a good snack or luncheon dish, but it may also be made into mini sandwiches and served hot with drinks or as a delicious appetiser.
Preheat Sandwich Toaster. Butter bread generously on 1 side of each slice. Beat egg and milk together until well blended, pour into a shallow dish. Dip unbuttered sides of 4 bread slices, 1 at a time, quickly into the egg and milk mixture. Drain for a moment on kitchen paper and place a slice of cheese onto the dipped side of the bread, top with a slice of ham. Dip and drain remaining bread slices, cover ham with dipped sides of bread. Place sandwiches in the scallops, close lid and cook for 2 minutes.
Note: If you want to make mini sandwiches remember to turn them after 1 minute.
Variation: Substitute thinly sliced chicken for the ham and cook as above.

Lox with a Difference

Serves 4-8

8 slices white milk bread
melted butter for brushing
90 g cream cheese
4 slices smoked salmon

Preheat Sandwich Toaster. Brush 1 side of the bread slices with melted butter. Beat cream cheese to soften it and divide between 4 slices of bread. Cover cheese with smoked salmon. Top with remaining bread buttered sides up, and cook for 2 minutes, turning sandwiches halfway through cooking time to make minis. Serve hot or cold.

Herring Canapés

Serves 8-10

16-20 thin slices white milk bread
60 g butter, melted
1 x 340-g jar rollmop herrings, cut
  into 1-cm strips
3 tablespoons mayonnaise
2 Granny Smith apples, peeled,
  cored and finely sliced
cucumber slices or bread and
  butter pickles for garnish

Preheat Sandwich Toaster. Trim crusts from bread and brush 1 side with melted butter. Cover half the bread, unbuttered sides, with rollmop pieces. Top rollmops with a layer of sliced apple. Spread unbuttered sides of remaining bread lightly with mayonnaise and cover canapes with these. Place in toaster and cook for 2 minutes, turning after 1 minute to cut into mini size. Serve cold, garnished with cucumber or pickles.
Note: The results are best when cooked in the Snackmaker or Sandwich Toaster.

Devils on Horseback
(Pictured on page 19)
Serves 6

6 rashers bacon, halved and rind
  removed
12 dessert prunes, pitted

Wrap Arounds and more hot tidbits to have with drinks. They are easy to make and there is no need for plates when serving them.
Preheat Sandwich Toaster. Wrap each prune in half a rasher of bacon, secure with a short piece of cocktail stick if necessary. Cook for 2-3 minutes or until bacon is crisp.
Note: If the Devils are well wrapped in bacon you will not need the cocktail sticks, just lay them join sides down in the scallops.

Angels on Horseback

Serves 6

12 fresh oysters
freshly ground black pepper
6 rashers bacon, halved and rind
  removed

Preheat Sandwich Toaster. Season oysters well with black pepper. Wrap each oyster in a half rasher of bacon and secure with a cocktail stick if necessary. Cook for 2-3 minutes or until bacon is crisp.

Angels in Saddle on Horseback

Serves 6

12 fresh oysters
cayenne pepper
12 anchovy fillets
6 rashers bacon, halved and rind removed

Preheat Sandwich Toaster. Sprinkle each oyster very lightly with cayenne pepper. Wrap 1 anchovy fillet around each oyster. Wrap half bacon rashers around wrapped oysters. Secure, if necessary, with short cocktail sticks. Cook for 2-3 minutes or until bacon is crisp.

Chicken Livers on Horseback

Serves 6

125 g chicken livers, trimmed
salt
freshly ground black pepper
6 rashers bacon, halved and rind removed

Preheat Sandwich Toaster. Season chicken livers with salt and freshly ground black pepper to taste. Wrap livers in bacon and secure with cocktail sticks. Cook for 2-3 minutes or until bacon is crisp.

Bareback Riders

Serves 6

12 shelled Brazil nuts
6 rashers bacon, halved and rind removed

Preheat Sandwich Toaster. Simply wrap each Brazil nut in half a bacon rasher, secure with a short cocktail stick and cook for 2 minutes or until bacon is crisp.
Variation: Roll each Brazil nut in curry powder before wrapping in bacon.

Red Riders

(Pictured on page 19)
Serves 6

12 mini frankfurters
6 rashers bacon, halved and rind removed

Preheat Sandwich Toaster. Wrap each frankfurter in half a bacon rasher, secure with a short cocktail stick and cook for 2-3 minutes or until bacon is crisp.

Black Knights

Serves 6

3 small frankfurters
12 dessert prunes, pitted
6 rashers bacon, halved and rind removed

Here is a variation of Wrap Arounds.
Preheat Sandwich Toaster. Quarter frankfurters and slip a piece into the centre of each prune. Wrap in bacon, secure with a cocktail stick and cook for 2-3 minutes or until the bacon is very crisp.
Variations: Fill prune centres with strips of ham, cooked chicken, pork or Cheddar cheese and wrap with bacon. Wrap any of the above filled prunes in salami, secure and cook for 1-2 minutes.

Sandwiches

Savoury or sweet, simple or elaborate, toasted sandwiches may be served on many occasions. Quick to prepare they are ideal for lunch or a snack.

The variety of sandwich fillings that may be used is endless. Choose from meats, poultry, fish, vegetables, fruits, cheeses, nuts or preserves or a combination of several. When using cheeses, avoid using the processed varieties since they will liquefy under high temperatures.

Canned or frozen convenience foods may be used alone or with fresh ingredients to add variety to the fillings and produce a tasty snack or meal. Of course, toasted sandwiches provide the ideal way to use leftovers. If there is insufficient filling available, use thick slices of bread to ensure an evenly browned sandwich.

Try using different types of bread and a Flavoured Butter (recipes start on page 100). Some protein enriched and black breads hardened when cooked but most of the breads on the market are suitable.

Garnish savoury sandwiches with parsley, mint, stuffed olive slices, tomato wedges or gherkin fans and serve them piping hot.

Sandwiches for all occasions

Sandwich Piquant

Serves 4

2 tablespoons tomato paste
2 teaspoons Worcestershire sauce
1 x 100-g can smoked oyster
   spread
8 slices wholemeal bread, buttered
   on 1 side
½ cabana sausage, thinly sliced
1 medium tomato, thinly sliced
90 g mozzarella cheese, grated
1 small onion, finely sliced
salt and pepper to taste

Preheat Sandwich Toaster. Mix tomato paste, Worcestershire sauce and smoked oyster spread together until thoroughly combined. Spread savoury mixture onto unbuttered sides of 4 bread slices. Divide cabana sausage between the sandwiches, cover with tomato, mozzarella cheese and onion. Season with salt and pepper. Top with remaining bread, buttered sides up, and cook for 2-3 minutes until crisp and golden.

Mrs Edna Klau, Box 150 P.O., Ceduna, S.A. 5690.

Gourmet Toasted Sandwiches

Serves 4

8 slices wholemeal bread, buttered
   on 1 side
1 x 95-g can liver pâté
4 rashers bacon, halved and lightly
   grilled
2 medium tomatoes, thinly sliced
freshly ground black pepper
2 teaspoons finely chopped parsley

Spread unbuttered sides of bread with generous layer of pâté. Preheat Sandwich Toaster. Place half the bread, buttered sides down, in toaster. Cover pâté with 4 halved rashers of bacon, top with tomato slices, season with pepper and a sprinkle of chopped parsley. Top with remaining bread, buttered sides up, and cook for 2 minutes.

Mrs E. Harrington, 7 Wight Street, Milton, Qld 4064.

Grapefruit and Salmon Slice

Serves 4-6

2 cups fresh grapefruit, cut into 5-
   mm slices
12 slices bread, buttered on 1 side
1 cup diced celery
¼ cup diced green capsicum
1 x 220-g can salmon, drained and
   flaked
salt and pepper to taste
¼ cup mayonnaise
pimiento strips for garnish

Preheat Sandwich Toaster. Place half the grapefruit onto unbuttered sides of bread, add celery, green capsicum and salmon. Season to taste with salt and pepper. Spread mayonnaise onto unbuttered sides of top bread slices. Cover with remaining bread, buttered sides up, and cook for 2 minutes. Serve hot garnished with pimiento strips and remaining grapefruit.

Mrs E. Beck, 74 Hawkers Road, Medindie, S.A. 5081.

Savoury Strasbourg Snacks

Serves 4

1 tablespoon melted butter for
   brushing
2 tablespoons butter or margarine,
   softened
½ teaspoon curry powder
8 slices white or wholemeal bread
2 tablespoons fruit chutney
4 thick slices pork Strasbourg
   sausage
4 slices Cheddar cheese

Preheat Sandwich Toaster, brushing thoroughly with melted butter. Beat softened butter or margarine with curry powder until well blended. Spread curried butter over 1 side of each slice of bread. Place bread in toaster, buttered sides up, top 4 slices with chutney, add sausage and cheese and finally top with remaining bread, buttered sides to the cheese. Place sandwiches in toaster and cook for 2 minutes or until crisp and golden.

Mrs G.B. Rogers, 7/2 Hazel Street, Ascot Park, S.A. 5043.

This plate of hors d'oeuvre — bite-sized delicacies to serve with drinks — demonstrates the versatility of the Snackmakers. The front plate shows Devils on Horseback (see page 15) and Red Riders (see page 16). The Sausage Rolls (see page 13) were turned in the scallops during the cooking time to give them an unusual shape; and the Cheese and Onion Puffs (see page 13) at the back, were turned across the centre cutters of the Snackmaker during the cooking time, thus making them the right size to eat easily with the fingers.

Chinese Breeze
(Pictured opposite)
Serves 4

2 eggs
½ cup milk
2 teaspoons dry sherry
2 teaspoons soy sauce
2 teaspoons vegetable oil
½ teaspoon sugar
salt and pepper to taste
melted butter for brushing
8 slices bread
6 shallots (spring onions), cut into
    5-mm slices
1 x 115-ml can champignons,
    drained and chopped
1 cup finely shredded cabbage
6 water chestnuts, finely chopped
1 cup diced cooked pork

Beat eggs with milk, sherry, soy sauce, oil, sugar, salt and pepper to taste. Brush scallops with melted butter and preheat Sandwich Toaster. Quickly dip 4 bread slices into egg mixture and place in Sandwich Toaster. Sprinkle dipped bread with shallots, champignons, cabbage, water chestnuts and pork. Dip remaining bread into egg and place on top of first slice. Cook for 2 minutes or until golden and crisp. Serve with sweet and sour sauce if liked.
Variations: Substitute 1 cup of chopped ham, cooked chicken or seafood instead of pork.

Ms J.V. Crisp, 27 Allowrie Street, Jamberoo, N.S.W. 2533.

Shanghai Surprise

Serves 4

125 g lean pork, finely minced
125 g green prawns, finely minced
2 shallots (spring onions), finely
    chopped
¼ teaspoon salt
2 teaspoons soy sauce
4 drops sesame oil
½ teaspoon sugar
pinch monosodium glutamate,
    optional
pinch black pepper
1 tablespoon vegetable oil
8 slices bread, buttered on 1 side

Combine all ingredients, except oil and bread. Heat oil in a shallow pan and fry the mixture until the prawns are pink and the pork is cooked. Preheat Sandwich Toaster. Lay bread, buttered sides down, into scallops, divide mixture between the 4 sandwiches, top with remaining bread, buttered sides up. Close lid and cook for 2 minutes. Serve hot or cold with Chinese plum sauce or hoisin sauce.
Variation: Use above filling in Puff Pastry (see page 52), and cook in preheated toaster for 4-5 minutes. Serve as above.

Mrs S. Wilson, 40 Moore Street, Roseville East, N.S.W. 2069.

Vienna Treats

Makes 1

2 slices Swiss cheese
2 slices bread, buttered on 1 side
1 frankfurter
mustard
barbecue sauce

Preheat Sandwich Toaster. Place 1 slice of cheese on the unbuttered side of a slice of bread. Cut frankfurter lengthways in halves. Place frankfurter on cheese. Spread frankfurter with mustard and add a little barbecue sauce if desired. Top with remaining cheese and bread, buttered side up. Cook for 2 minutes.

Chinese Breeze, crisp Chinese-style sandwiches (see above), are filled with chopped vegetables and prawns, a variation on the basic recipe. The ingredients are shown in the bowl at left. Cook in a Snackmaker or Sandwich Toaster and serve them with sweet and sour sauce.

German Toasted Cheese

Serves 4

8 slices wholemeal bread
melted butter for brushing
2 tablespoons Dijon mustard
⅓ cup beer
1 cup grated Cheddar cheese

Preheat Sandwich Toaster. Brush 1 side of each bread slice lightly with melted butter. Place mustard in a small bowl and gradually add the beer and cheese. Spread onto unbuttered sides of 4 bread slices, top with remaining bread, buttered sides up, and cook for 2 minutes or until crisp. Serve with broccoli pieces which have been lightly buttered and sprinkled with a little lemon juice.
Note: Not suitable for Electric Jaffle.

Chicken Luau

Serves 2

4 slices bread
¼ cup chopped, cooked chicken
¼ cup drained, crushed pineapple
¼ cup finely chopped celery
1 tablespoon mayonnaise
pinch ground ginger
salt and pepper to taste

Preheat Sandwich Toaster. Butter 1 side of each bread slice. Combine all ingredients. Spread mixture on unbuttered sides of bread, top with remaining slices, buttered sides up, and cook for 2 minutes or until golden.

Mrs B. Ryan, 5 Abermere Avenue, Mt Stuart, Tas. 7000.

Simon's Silly Chilli

Serves 4-6

1 large brown onion, finely
** chopped**
1 clove garlic, crushed
2 tablespoons safflower oil
500 g minced topside
1 teaspoon Mexican chilli powder
¼ teaspoon turmeric
¼ teaspoon ground cumin
1 bay leaf
2 large tomatoes, sliced
½ cup tomato sauce
1 beef stock cube, dissolved in
** ½ cup hot water**
salt and pepper to taste
8-12 slices wholemeal bread,
** buttered on 1 side**
½ cup sour cream

Fry the onion and garlic in oil until lightly browned. Add minced beef and cook until colour changes, combine well with onions and garlic. Stir in chilli powder, turmeric, cumin, bay leaf and tomatoes and mix thoroughly. Cook for 2-3 minutes and add tomato sauce and beef stock. Stir well, correct seasoning and reduce temperature to simmer. Cook for a minimum of 30 minutes. Preheat Sandwich Toaster. Place half the bread, buttered sides down, in toaster. Place approximately a third cup of chilli mixture onto each slice of bread, top with remaining bread, buttered sides up and cook for 2 minutes. Serve hot with a crisp green salad. Garnish with sour cream.
Note: The quantities can easily be doubled and Simon's Silly Chilli will keep well, covered, in the refrigerator for several days. More (or less) chilli powder can be added according to taste.

Mr S. Eyland, 162 Belgrave Esplanade, Sylvania Waters, N.S.W. 2224.

Poor Boy Sandwich

Serves 4

8 slices sourdough bread, buttered
    on 1 side
1 tablespoon mayonnaise
1 medium tomato, thinly sliced
½ teaspoon dried tarragon
2 hard-boiled eggs, sliced
12 slices cucumber
salt and freshly ground black
    pepper
1 shallot (spring onion), cut into
    fine rings
16 thin slices salami
4 slices Swiss cheese
4 thin slices prosciutto or ham

This is really anything but poor; it originated in France when poor boys would knock on doors asking for food and were given whatever was available in the house. Toasted, the Poor Boy Sandwich is a meal in itself.
Preheat Sandwich Toaster. Place 4 slices of bread buttered sides down. Spread lightly with mayonnaise and layer the ingredients in given order. Top with remaining bread, buttered sides up, and cook for 2 minutes or until crisp and golden. Serve with Potato Salad (see page 91). **Note**: Sourdough bread is traditionally used for this sandwich and is very good but any bread of your choice can be used.

Gypsy Sandwich

Serves 4

8 slices bread
butter
1 cup grated tasty Cheddar cheese
1 small onion, finely chopped
¼ cup mayonnaise
1 small green capsicum, seeded
    and finely chopped
½ teaspoon curry powder
2 teaspoons white vinegar
12 green olives, pitted and roughly
    chopped

Preheat Sandwich Toaster. Butter bread on 1 side only. Combine remaining ingredients. Spread mixture on unbuttered sides of 4 slices of bread and top with remaining slices, buttered sides up. Cook for 2 minutes or until golden brown. Delicious with Waldorf Salad (see page 92).

Sizzling Seafood Pasties

Serves 4

1 small onion, finely chopped
60 g mushrooms, chopped
15 g butter or margarine
1 x 105-g can salmon, drained and
    flaked
1 x 90-g can prawns, drained
1 hard-boiled egg, chopped
pinch cayenne pepper
2 tablespoons sour cream
salt and pepper to taste
½ teaspoon chopped chives
1 tablespoon dry white wine
4 tablespoons Parmesan cheese
8 slices bread, buttered on 1 side
tomato wedges and celery to
    garnish

Saute onion and mushrooms in butter until tender, set aside. Mix together salmon, prawns, egg, cayenne pepper and sour cream, season to taste with salt and pepper and chives. Combine onion mixture with fish mixture, stir in wine and chill. When ready to serve, preheat Sandwich Toaster, sprinkle unbuttered sides of 4 bread slices with 2 teaspoons of Parmesan cheese each. Spread a generous layer of fish mixture onto bread and sprinkle 2 more teaspoons Parmesan onto each sandwich filling. Top with remaining bread, buttered sides up, and cook for 2-3 minutes or until golden brown and sizzling. Serve hot garnished with tomato and celery.

Ms Tina Gibson, 60 McIntosh Road, Narraweena, N.S.W. 2099.

Piperade

Serves 4-6

1 tablespoon oil
60 g butter
1 large onion, finely sliced
1 green capsicum, cored and diced
1 red capsicum, cored and diced
1 large tomato, peeled and
  chopped
1 tablespoon mixed fresh herbs
salt and pepper to taste
3 eggs, lightly beaten
8-12 slices milk bread, buttered on
  1 side

This mixture of vegetables and eggs is a good combination, either as a sandwich filling or chilled as a salad.
Heat the oil in a frying pan with half the butter, add the onion and capsicums, and cook over medium heat for 3-4 minutes. Add tomato, reduce heat and cook gently for a further 4-5 minutes or until vegetables are tender but not mushy. Remove from heat, add herbs and season to taste with salt and pepper. Melt remaining butter and cook the eggs, seasoned with salt and pepper, until just set, but still creamy. Remove from heat and cool. Combine the 2 mixtures. Preheat Sandwich Toaster. Spread unbuttered sides of half the slices of bread with Piperade. Cover with remaining bread slices, buttered sides up. Cook for 2 minutes and serve with grilled ham steaks.
Note: If fresh herbs are not available 1 teaspoon of mixed dried herbs can be substituted.
Variation: Chill Piperade and serve as a salad with a toasted sandwich of your choice.

Herbed Tomato Snack

Serves 1

2 slices bread, white, wholemeal or
  wholegrain
butter
1 tablespoon cream cheese
1 small tomato, thinly sliced
2 teaspoons Herb Butter (see page
  100) or ½ teaspoon chopped
  fresh basil
salt and pepper to taste

Preheat Sandwich Toaster. Butter 1 side of each bread slice. Spread unbuttered side of 1 slice of bread with the cream cheese and the unbuttered side of the second bread slice with Herb Butter, if using. Place first slice of bread, buttered side down, into scallop. Add a layer of tomato slices and season with salt and pepper. If not using the Herb Butter sprinkle fresh basil onto the tomatoes. Cover with remaining bread, buttered side up, and cook for 2 minutes or until crisp and golden.

Curried Salmon Snack

Makes 6

1 x 220-g can salmon, drained
  and flaked
1 teaspoon curry powder
1 small onion, finely chopped
½ cup chopped celery
30 g cheese, grated
2 tablespoons butter
2 tablespoons flour
1 cup milk
salt and pepper to taste
12 slices bread, buttered on 1 side

Combine salmon, curry powder, onion, celery and cheese. Melt butter, stir in flour and cook for 1 minute, stirring continually. Gradually stir in milk and cook until sauce boils and thickens. Season with salt and pepper. Place slices of bread into preheated Sandwich Toaster, buttered sides down. Place third cup of mixture onto each bread slice. Top with slices of bread, buttered sides up. Lower lid and cook for 2 minutes.

Salmon and Cucumber

Serves 1

2 slices brown bread
butter
1½ tablespoons canned salmon,
    drained and flaked
6 slices cucumber
1 teaspoon chopped chives
mayonnaise

Preheat Sandwich Toaster. Butter 1 side of each bread slice. Spread salmon on unbuttered side of 1 bread slice. Cover salmon with cucumber slices, sprinkle with chives and small dabs of mayonnaise. Top with remaining slice of bread, buttered side up, and cook for 2 minutes or until crisp.

Dressy Baked Bean Special

Serves 4

8 slices brown or white milk bread
butter
1 x 225-g can baked beans
1 tablespoon honey
1 tablespoon molasses
1 small onion, grated or finely
    chopped
salt and pepper to taste

A baked bean sandwich, the children's favourite, becomes a special treat when cooked this way.
Preheat Sandwich Toaster. Butter 1 side of each slice of bread. Combine beans with honey, molasses and grated onion. Season to taste with salt and pepper. Place half the bread buttered sides down into toaster. Divide mixture between the slices and top with remaining bread, buttered sides up. Close toaster and cook for 2 minutes or until crisp and golden.
Note: Served with crisply fried bacon rashers, this makes a nutritious breakfast or snack.

Camembert Special

Serves 4

8 slices brown or white milk bread
melted butter for brushing
1 baby Camembert cheese

This is simple and delicious. Make a special snack for yourself, serve them with a salad for lunch or make mini sandwiches for your guests.
Preheat Sandwich Toaster. Brush 1 side of each bread slice with butter. Cut Camembert into quarters and spread cheese evenly over 4 slices of bread. Top with remaining bread, buttered sides up. Cook for 2-2½ minutes. Serve very hot.

Smoked Cheese Special

Serves 1

2 slices white bread
butter
1 slice German smoked cheese
1 slice ham
4 slices Granny Smith apple

This is an old favourite with a difference.
Preheat Sandwich Toaster. Butter 1 side of each bread slice. Lay cheese on unbuttered side of bread, cover with ham and apple slices. Add remaining bread, buttered side up, and cook for 2 minutes.
Note: Any smoked cheese would suffice but the German one has a particularly good flavour.

Zucchini Savoury

Makes 2

4 slices bread, buttered on 1 side
1 zucchini, finely sliced
60 g tasty cheese, grated
2 slices salami
salt and pepper

Place 2 slices of bread, buttered sides down, into preheated Sandwich Toaster. Place zucchini, cheese and salami onto bread, sprinkle with salt and pepper. Top with bread, buttered sides up. Cook for 2 minutes.

Zucchini and Bacon Snacks

Serves 4

8 slices bread, buttered on 1 side
8 medium zucchini, thinly sliced
salt and freshly ground black
　　pepper
4 rashers bacon, with rind
　　removed, cut into 1-cm strips
¼-½ teaspoon granulated garlic

Preheat Sandwich Toaster. Lay zucchini slices onto unbuttered sides of bread slices, sprinkle lightly with salt, place bacon strips over zucchini and season with pepper and granulated garlic to taste. Top with remaining bread, buttered sides up. Place in toaster and cook for 2 minutes.

Mrs W. Anderson, 'Palomar', Broomehill, W.A. 6318.

Corn and Bacon Snacks

Makes 1

1 rasher bacon, chopped and fried
　　(reserve bacon dripping)
1 tablespoon creamed corn
1 tablespoon grated cheese
salt and pepper
2 slices bread

Combine bacon, corn, cheese, salt and pepper. Dip bread in bacon dripping and place 1 slice dripping side down onto Sandwich Toaster. Form a hollow with the back of a spoon and add filling. Top with remaining slice of bread, dripping side up. Lower lid and cook for 2 minutes.

Egg sandwiches

Nutritious and versatile, eggs may be cooked and served alone or with complementary additions which extend their flavour and variety of uses. A basic egg sandwich makes a quick, nourishing and easy-to-prepare breakfast. Add an extra ingredient and it becomes an any-time-of-day snack. With a salad it becomes a meal which is well balanced in protein, fats, carbohydrates, minerals and vitamins.

Egg Sandwiches

For each serve allow:

**2 slices white or brown bread,
    buttered on 1 side**
1 x 50-g egg, lightly beaten
salt and pepper to taste

Preheat Electric Jaffle, Snackmaker, or Sandwich Toaster. Season egg with salt and pepper. Place bread, buttered side down, into scallop. Make a small depression in the centre (or at either side of cutter), with the back of a spoon and pour in the egg mixture. Top with remaining bread, buttered side up. Close lid and cook for 2 minutes or until sandwich is crisp and golden.
Variations: Add any of the following to the beaten egg before cooking:
2 teaspoons chives, finely snipped
2 teaspoons parsley, finely chopped
1 tablespoon cheese, grated
3 stuffed olives, chopped
1 small slice ham, chopped
1 anchovy fillet, chopped
1 small rasher bacon, crisply fried and crumbled
Note: If using Electric Jaffle for 1 person, use bread of toasting thickness or 60-g egg.

Creoled Eggs

Serves 2

**4 slices white or brown bread,
    buttered on 1 side**
1 small onion
½ stick celery
¼ small green capsicum
**2 teaspoons tomato paste or
    tomato sauce**
salt and pepper to taste
2 eggs

You will need a blender or Kitchen Wizz for this dish. Use an Electric Jaffle for the whole eggs. See note.
Preheat Electric Jaffle. Place roughly chopped onion, celery and capsicum into blender or Kitchen Wizz and purée. Mix the vegetable purée with tomato paste or sauce and season to taste with salt and pepper. Spread mixture on unbuttered sides of the bread. Lay 2 slices, buttered sides down, into Electric Jaffle and make a depression in the centres, using the back of a spoon. Add the eggs and top with remaining bread slices, buttered sides up. Close and cook for 2-2½ minutes.
Note: This can be made in the Sandwich Toaster but use small eggs and lightly beat them into the vegetable mixture before filling the sandwiches.

New Orleans Eggs

Serves 1

**2 slices brown or white toasting
  bread**
butter
1 x 50-55-g egg
salt and pepper to taste
**2 teaspoons grated Cheddar
  cheese**
¼ teaspoon Worcestershire sauce

Preheat Electric Jaffle. Lightly butter both sides of the
bread and lay 1 slice in the scallop making a depression in
the centre with the back of a spoon. Break the egg into
the depression, season with salt and pepper and sprinkle
the cheese over the top. Splash with Worcestershire
sauce, cover with the remaining bread slice, close lid and
cook for 2 minutes. Serve hot, alone or with a crisp salad.

Scalloped Eggs

Serves 2

4 slices white bread
melted butter for brushing
**1-2 tablespoons golden crumbs or
  corn flake crumbs**
3 hard-boiled eggs, sliced
2 tablespoons cream
salt and pepper to taste
2 slices ham

Preheat Electric Jaffle or Snackmaker. Brush 1 side of
each bread slice with melted butter and dip the buttered
sides into the crumbs. The bread should be only lightly
crumbed. Place 2 slices, crumbed sides down, into the
scallops. Divide the sliced eggs between the scallops and
drizzle cream over the eggs. Season with salt and plenty
of pepper. Top with ham slices and the remaining bread,
crumbed sides up. Close toaster and cook for 2 minutes
or until crisp and golden. Very good either hot or cold.
Variation: Replace ham with 2 tablespoons chopped
cooked chicken or shellfish.

Muffin Eggs
(Pictured opposite)
Serves 1

1 English-style muffin
melted butter for brushing
1 small egg
salt and pepper to taste

Preheat Electric Jaffle. Split muffin through the centre
and remove a little of the bread from each half. Brush
both sides of the muffin halves with melted butter. Place
half a muffin into the scallop, carefully break the egg on
top and season with salt and pepper. Top with remaining
half muffin, close lid and cook for 2-2½ minutes.

*Muffin Eggs (see above) are perfect for breakfast. Simply top
the raw egg with the remaining muffin half and cook in minutes
using an Electric Jaffle.*

Children's own
and sandwiches for one

A group of children, when offered a wide range of breads and fresh and canned foods, concocted this collection of sandwich fillings and tested them. Generally they disregarded the usual children's favourites and chose surprisingly sophisticated combinations which not only taste good but are nutritious too. Without being told, in most cases they added at least 1 ingredient to give texture or crunch to their sandwiches, and they all preferred them when made into mini sandwiches. The minimum amount of crust was removed from the bread and in only 1 recipe the bread is buttered on both sides.
The children's adventure in sandwich making, has created recipes for toasted treats which are very suitable for single serves for 1 person. With the addition of a salad or soup most of these sandwiches will provide a convenient and adequate meal if you are eating alone or you don't wish to prepare an elaborate dish.

Dried Fruit Medley
(Pictured opposite)
Serves 1

2 slices white bread
butter
1 teaspoon peanut butter
1 tablespoon mixed dried fruit
(sultanas, currants, raisins)
1 tablespoon bean sprouts or
shredded lettuce
2 teaspoons pine nuts
4 thin slices Granny Smith apple
2 potato crisps

Preheat Sandwich Toaster. Butter bread on 1 side. Lightly spread peanut butter onto unbuttered side of 1 bread slice. Mix together dried fruit, bean sprouts and nuts. Press fruit mixture onto peanut butter. Lay apple slices over the fruit and top with potato crisps. Cover with remaining bread slice, buttered side up. Cook for 2 minutes.
Note: Any nuts can be used instead of pine nuts.

The little square shapes for Dried Fruit Medley (see above) were made by turning the sandwiches across the cutters of the Snackmaker during cooking time.

Tuna Salad

Serves 1

2 slices white bread
butter
1 tablespoon canned tuna and
   onion
¼ stick celery, finely sliced
1 tablespoon alfalfa sprouts or
   shredded lettuce
4 thin slices Granny Smith apple

Preheat Sandwich Toaster. Butter 1 side of each bread slice. Spread the unbuttered side of 1 slice of bread with tuna and onion. Cover with sliced celery, alfalfa sprouts or lettuce and lay sliced apple on top. Cover with remaining bread, buttered side up, and cook for 2 minutes.
Note: If using Snackmaker or Sandwich Toaster turn sandwich after 1 minute to make mini sandwiches.

Prawn and Tomato Treat

Serves 1

2 slices brown bread
butter
1½ tablespoons cooked prawns,
   fresh or canned
4 slices tomato, cut into 3-mm
   rounds
salt to taste
mayonnaise

This is the only recipe in which the children added salt. Preheat Sandwich Toaster. Butter bread lightly on both sides. Spread prawns evenly over 1 piece of bread. Cover with tomato slices and season with salt. Spread mayonnaise onto top slice of bread and close sandwich, mayonnaise side onto tomatoes. Cook for 2 minutes or until crisp and golden.

Appled Pork and Ham

Serves 1

1 slice white milk bread
1 slice brown milk bread
butter
1 tablespoon apple sauce
2 slices pork and ham loaf
1 shallot (spring onion), cut into
   5-mm rings

The mixture of breads in this sandwich gives added interest, but they do have to be the same size.
Preheat Sandwich Toaster. Butter 1 side of each bread slice. Spread unbuttered side of 1 slice with apple sauce, cover with pork and ham loaf and sprinkle with shallots. Top with remaining slice of bread buttered side up. Close toaster and cook for 2 minutes or until crisp and golden.

Ham and Sweetcorn

Serves 1

2 slices white bread
butter
1 tablespoon creamed sweetcorn
1 slice ham
1 tablespoon shredded lettuce
1 tablespoon finely chopped chives

Preheat Sandwich Toaster. Butter bread on 1 side. Spread unbuttered side of 1 slice with creamed sweetcorn. Top with ham, lettuce and chives. Top with remaining slice of bread, buttered side up, and cook for 2 minutes.

Salami Crunch Sandwich

Serves 1

2 slices brown bread
butter
4 slices salami
4 slices apple
1 tablespoon grated carrot
1 tablespoon finely sliced celery

Preheat Sandwich Toaster. Butter bread on 1 side. Lay salami on unbuttered side of 1 slice, cover with apple, grated carrot and celery slices. Top with remaining bread, buttered side up, and cook for 2 minutes.

Chicken Cheese Salad Surprise

Serves 1

2 slices brown bread
butter
2 teaspoons mayonnaise
1 tablespoon finely diced, cooked
  chicken
4 slices hard-boiled egg
2 teaspoons grated Cheddar
  cheese
2 asparagus spears
8 canned mandarin segments
sprinkling sprouted fenugreek

This combination makes use of small amounts of many ingredients. The addition of mandarin segments gives a surprising flavour.
Preheat Sandwich Toaster. Butter 1 side of each bread slice. Spread unbuttered side of bread lightly with mayonnaise. Onto bottom slice of bread, spread diced chicken. Cover with egg slices and sprinkle over the cheese. Lay on top the asparagus, mandarins and fenugreek sprouts. Top with remaining bread, mayonnaise side down. Cook for 2 minutes or until crisp and golden.
Note: Three varieties of sprouted beans were offered to the children, as well as shredded lettuce. Without exception they preferred the bean sprouts but lettuce can be substituted.

Pineapple Cheese Sandwich

Serves 1

2 slices brown bread
butter
1 tablespoon cream cheese
1 tablespoon crushed and drained
  pineapple
2 teaspoons pine nuts
sprinkling of finely chopped
  parsley

Preheat Sandwich Toaster. Butter 1 side of each bread slice and spread unbuttered side of 1 slice with cream cheese. Top cheese with pineapple, pine nuts and parsley. Cover with remaining bread buttered side up. Cook for 2 minutes.
Note: Pine nuts are very good with this mixture but any nuts may be substituted.

Chinese Chip Buttie

Serves 1

2 slices white bread, buttered on 1
  side
1 tablespoon diced, cooked
  chicken
4-5 large potato crisps, lightly
  crushed
1 scant tablespoon finely sliced
  celery
1 tablespoon bean sprouts, fresh
  or canned

This was the most favoured sandwich of all the combinations and all the children liked the taste.
Preheat Sandwich Toaster. Spread chicken over the unbuttered side of 1 slice of bread. Sprinkle with potato chips, celery and bean sprouts. Cover with remaining bread, buttered side up, and cook for 2 minutes or until crisp and golden.
Note: If using canned bean sprouts they must be well drained.

Carrot and Peanut Sandwich

Serves 1

2 slices brown bread
butter
1 teaspoon mayonnaise
1 tablespoon grated carrot
1 tablespoon chopped salted
  peanuts
2 midget dill pickles, sliced

Preheat Sandwich Toaster. Lightly butter bread on 1 side. Spread unbuttered side of 1 slice with mayonnaise. Cover mayonnaise with carrot and sprinkle with chopped peanuts and pickles. Top with remaining slice, buttered side up, close toaster and cook for 2 minutes.
Variation: Replace dill pickles with 1 tablespoon seedless raisins.

Pineapple Date Delight

Serves 1

2 slices white bread
butter
1 tablespoon crushed and
drained pineapple
4 dates, pitted and chopped
1 tablespoon sliced celery

Preheat Sandwich Toaster. Butter 1 side of each bread slice. Spread drained pineapple on unbuttered side of 1 slice of bread. Top with chopped dates and celery. Cover with remaining bread slice buttered side up and cook for 2 minutes or until crisp and golden.

Banana Nut Cream

Serves 1

2 slices brown bread
butter
peanut butter
1 small banana, mashed
2 teaspoons sour cream
½ teaspoon sugar, optional

Preheat Sandwich Toaster. Lightly butter bread on 1 side. Spread a thin layer of peanut butter on unbuttered sides of bread slices. Cover 1 side with mashed banana, top with sour cream and a sprinkling of sugar. Cover with remaining bread, buttered side up, and cook for 2 minutes or until crisp and golden.
Variation: Rhubarb Nut Cream. Replace banana with 2 tablespoons cooked fresh rhubarb or canned rhubarb which has been well drained.

Using leftovers

What can be done with those very small amounts of leftover fish, meat or chicken, that are too much to throw away and often end up as a gourmet meal for the family's pet? Make a toasted sandwich and transform leftovers into a worthwhile snack or quick meal.

Castaway Luau

Serves 2

½ cup flaked, cooked fish
½ teaspoon rum
1 small onion, finely sliced
½ teaspoon finely chopped parsley
½ teaspoon lemon juice
¼ cup diced pawpaw
salt and pepper to taste
4 slices smoked processed cheese
4 slices bread, buttered on 1 side

Combine fish, rum, onion, parsley, lemon juice and pawpaw. Season to taste with salt and pepper. Preheat Sandwich Toaster. Lay a slice of cheese on the unbuttered sides of 2 slices of bread. Divide fish mixture between the 2 slices, cover mixture with remaining cheese slices and top with remaining bread, buttered sides up. Cook for 2 minutes or until crisp and golden. Serve hot garnished with lemon wedges and Tartare Sauce (see page 99).
Note: This is particularly good when made with wholemeal bread.

Ms R.I. Benson, Box 48, Red Hill, Qld 4059.

Florentine Fish

Serves 4

8 slices white or brown bread
melted butter for brushing
250 g cooked boneless fish, flaked
½ x 375-g packet frozen spinach, thawed
1 small onion, grated
3 tablespoons cream
salt and pepper to taste
60 g Cheddar cheese, grated
1 medium tomato, finely sliced
pinch paprika pepper

Preheat Sandwich Toaster. Brush bread slices with butter on 1 side. Combine flaked fish with spinach, grated onion and cream. Season to taste with salt and pepper. Place 4 slices of bread, buttered sides down into toaster scallops. Divide fish mixture between the scallops, sprinkle lightly with grated cheese, top with sliced tomato and season with paprika and salt and pepper. Close toaster and cook for 2-2½ minutes. Serve hot with a crisp green salad or vegetable of choice.
Note: Almost any cooked fish can be used.
Variation: Florentine Pies. Replace bread slices with 1 quantity of Shortcrust Pastry (see page 53). Roll pastry to a thickness of 3 mm. Cut to fit scallops and fill with above mixture.

Veal with Tuna Fish Sauce

Serves 4

8 slices white bread
melted butter for brushing
8 thin slices cooked veal
1 small tin anchovy fillets, drained
salt and pepper to taste
2-3 teaspoons lemon juice
1 x 110-g can tuna, drained and
    flaked
⅓ cup mayonnaise

Leftover veal can be tasteless when served alone. Try this adaptation of the classic Vitello Tonnato, served hot or cold.
Brush both sides of the bread with melted butter. Place a slice of veal onto 4 pieces of bread. Reserve 3 anchovy fillets and chop the rest. Divide chopped anchovies between the 4 sandwiches, lay another slice of veal over the anchovies and season lightly with salt and pepper. Close sandwiches with remaining bread. Preheat Sandwich Toaster.
Blend the reserved anchovies with lemon juice and flaked tuna, pounding them well together or mashing with the back of a spoon. Blend fish mixture into the mayonnaise and set aside.
Place sandwiches into toaster and cook for 2 minutes or until golden. Serve hot or chilled with the sauce handed separately.
Note: Broccoli is a very complementary accompaniment to this dish when it is served hot.

Christmas Turkey Delicious

Serves 4

8 slices bread, buttered on 1 side
2 tablespoons turkey stuffing
    (seasoning)
90 g cooked turkey, minced or
    finely diced
2 tablespoons chutney
salt and pepper to taste

When the Christmas turkey carcass is almost finished and everyone is thoroughly tired of turkey, this is a lovely way to serve the remnants.
Preheat Sandwich Toaster. Spread unbuttered sides of 4 slices of the bread with turkey seasoning (stuffing). Lay the 4 seasoned slices into the toaster, buttered sides down. Divide chopped turkey between the sandwiches and top with chutney. Season with salt and pepper. Top with remaining bread, buttered sides up and cook. Serve hot with Green Beans Almandine (see page 93) or vegetable of choice.
Note: This mixture is very suitable as mini sandwiches.
Variation: Substitute 90 g cooked chicken for turkey.

Turkey Divan

Serves 4

1 cup diced, cooked turkey
1 cup cooked broccoli
2 tablespoons cream or
    mayonnaise
¼ cup slivered almonds
salt and pepper to taste
1 tablespoon grated Parmesan
    cheese
8 slices bread, buttered on 1 side

Preheat Sandwich Toaster. Mix all ingredients together and divide between 4 slices of bread. Top with remaining slices, buttered sides up, and cook for 2 minutes. Serve with a crisp green salad.
Variation: 1 cup of cooked chicken can be substituted for the turkey meat.

Turkish Lamb

Serves 4

1½ cups cooked, diced lamb
3 tablespoons natural yoghurt
salt and pepper to taste
¼-½ teaspoon dried mixed herbs
8 slices bread, buttered on 1 side
2 tablespoons tomato paste

Preheat Sandwich Toaster. Combine lamb with yoghurt, salt and pepper and herbs. Spread 8 slices of bread lightly with tomato paste on the unbuttered sides. Divide filling between 4 bread slices, spreading the filling over the tomato paste. Cover with remaining bread, buttered sides up. Cook for 2-2½ minutes or until crisp and golden. Serve with a Tabbouleh Salad (see page 91).
Note: This filling also tastes good in filo or puff pastry. If using filo pastry, mix tomato paste with the filling ingredients and use filo in layers of 6.

Beef and Beetroot Snack

Serves 4

15 g butter
1 tablespoon finely chopped onion
2 teaspoons flour
½ cup plain yoghurt
1 cup grated cooked beetroot
1 teaspoon prepared horseradish
salt and pepper to taste
pinch sugar, optional
4 slices cooked beef or corned beef
8 slices bread, buttered on 1 side

Melt butter in frying-pan and fry onion until transparent, stir in flour and combine thoroughly. Add yoghurt stirring constantly until sauce thickens. Add beetroot and horseradish, season to taste adding a little sugar or more yoghurt if desired. Preheat Sandwich Toaster. Lay 1 slice of beef or corned beef onto unbuttered sides of bread, divide beetroot mixture between the slices and top with remaining bread, buttered sides up. Place in toaster and cook for 4-5 minutes or until golden brown.

Mrs D. Harris, 33 Wilsons Drive, Colo Vale, N.S.W. 2575.

Salad Sandwich

Any leftover salad can be used as a delicious filling for a sandwich. Try Mushroom Salad (see page 91) or Waldorf Salad (see page 92). Drain any excess dressing from salad. Preheat Sandwich Toaster. Butter bread on 1 side only. Place salad on unbuttered side of bread and cover with remaining bread, buttered side up. Cook for 2 minutes until crisp and golden.

Sandwiches as dessert

Breads have been used in traditional dessert recipes for countless years and many of these desserts can be made very easily in the Sandwich Toaster, Snackmaker or Electric Jaffle. There are also some new recipes to try.

After Dinner Delights

Serves 4-8

1 cup marshmallows, halved
½ cup sweet sherry
8 slices bread, buttered on 1 side
1 x 470-g can apricot halves, well drained
icing sugar for dusting
whipped cream, optional

Soak marshmallows in sherry for at least 2 hours or overnight. When ready to cook, preheat Sandwich Toaster and drain any excess syrup from marshmallow mixture. Place 2 or 4 slices of bread, buttered sides down, into Sandwich Toaster, making a hollow in the bread with the back of a spoon. Place 2 apricot halves into each scallop. Top apricots with marshmallow mixture and cover with remaining bread, buttered sides up. Cook for 2 minutes and serve hot or cold, lightly dusted with icing sugar and accompanied by whipped cream if liked.
Variation: Add 1 cup of well-drained, crushed pineapple to marshmallow mixture instead of apricots.

Mrs J. Arnold, 190 South Street, Windale, N.S.W. 2306.

Apple Charlotte
(See photograph on page 47)
Serves 4

8 slices white or fruit and nut bread, crusts removed
melted butter for brushing
1¼ cups canned pie apple or stewed apples
1 tablespoon lemon juice
½ teaspoon ground cinnamon

This method of making Apple Charlotte is quick, easy and it tastes as good as when it is made in the more conventional way.
Brush both sides of bread slices generously with melted butter. Set aside. Combine apple with lemon juice and cinnamon. The apple should be fairly tart but a little sugar may be added to taste. Preheat Sandwich Toaster. Lay 4 bread slices in scallops and divide apple mixture between them. Top with remaining bread and cook for 2-3 minutes. The bread should be crisply golden. Serve cold with whipped cream or they are especially good served hot with Apricot Sauce or Rasberry Sauce (see pages 97 and 98).
Note: For larger serves make Apple Charlotte using an Electric Jaffle.

Austrian Delight

Serves 2-4

4 slices white bread
butter
2 tablespoons sour cream
½ cup drained, chopped
    canned peaches
1 tablespoon brown sugar
½ teaspoon ground cinnamon
whipped cream or ice cream to
    serve

Preheat Sandwich Toaster. Butter bread on 1 side. Combine sour cream, peaches, sugar and cinnamon. Place 2 slices of bread, buttered sides down, into Sandwich Toaster. Divide filling between the 2, top with remaining bread, buttered sides up. Close toaster and cook for 2 minutes or until crisp and golden. Serve hot with cream or ice cream.

Banana Caramel Munchie

Serves 4

1 packet pancake or pikelet mix
8 slices fruit loaf or Shiraz fruit
    loaf, crusts removed
4 medium bananas, sliced
    lengthways
1 small carton caramel sauce
non-stick cooking spray

Make pancake or pikelet mix according to packet instructions. Place sliced bananas on 4 bread slices which have not been buttered. Using a teaspoon dipped into hot water, pour 1 teaspoon of caramel sauce over the bananas. Top with remaining unbuttered bread and using a fork and spoon to lift sandwich, dip each 1 into pancake mixture making sure sides are well coated. Place each sandwich onto a plate or rack to drain until coating is completed. Spray preheated Sandwich Toaster thoroughly with cooking spray and cook sandwiches in toaster for 1-1½ minutes. Serve plain or with ice cream or fresh cream or simply sprinkled with caster sugar.
Variation: Mincemeat Munchie. Mix 1 cup fruit mincemeat with 1 tablespoon brandy, rum or Grand Marnier. Use to fill sandwiches before coating in pancake mixture.

Mrs A.M. Bradley, 67 Telopea Street, Collaroy Plateau, N.S.W. 2098.

Blueberry Beauties

Serves 4

125 g butter, softened
½ cup honey
2 teaspoons grated orange rind
1 x 425-g can blueberries, drained
8 large marshmallows, chopped
8 slices bread, buttered on 1 side

Preheat Sandwich Toaster. Beat softened butter, honey and orange rind together and spread over unbuttered sides of bread. Top each with drained blueberries and chopped marshmallows. Close sandwiches with remaining bread and cook for 2 minutes.
Note: Marshmallows are most easily chopped using kitchen scissors.

Mrs Sylvia Stibbs, 46 Hunter Street, Wonthaggi, Vic. 3995.

Black Cherry Delight

Serves 3-4

6-8 slices bread, buttered on 1 side

Filling

125 g cream cheese
½ teaspoon grated lemon rind
1 tablespoon sugar
¼ cup plain yoghurt
2 teaspoons rum or brandy
1 x 440-g can black cherries

Sauce

30 g butter or margarine
2 tablespoons sugar
2 tablespoons rum or brandy
1 teaspoon lemon juice
**1 cup cherry syrup mixed with 1
  teaspoon cornflour**

Prepare filling and sauce in advance.

Filling

Combine cream cheese, lemon rind and sugar in a bowl, beat until creamy. Fold yoghurt and rum or brandy into cheese mixture. Drain and stone cherries, reserving the syrup. Add cherries to cheese mixture and set aside.

Sauce

Melt butter or margarine with sugar and stir until mixture bubbles. Add rum or brandy and flame. Shake pan gently and add lemon juice. When flames die down add cherry liquid, stirring constantly until mixture thickens. Reduce heat and simmer for 5 minutes.
When ready to serve, preheat Sandwich Toaster. Place bread, buttered sides down in toaster. Divide filling between slices, top with remaining slices, buttered sides up, and cook for 2 minutes or until golden. Serve hot, topped with Cherry Sauce.

Mrs Pam Newton, 92 Irvine Street, Watson, A.C.T. 2602.

Caramelised Pineapple

Serves 2

2 tablespoons softened butter
2 tablespoons brown sugar
**4 slices raisin bread, lightly
  buttered on 1 side**
2 slices pineapple, drained

Preheat Sandwich Toaster. Cream together the softened butter and brown sugar and spread on the unbuttered sides of the raisin bread. Cut pineapple slices into halves through the centre and place 2 pieces on each slice of bread. Top with remaining bread, buttered sides up, place in toaster and cook for 2 minutes.

French Toast

Serves 2

1 x 60-g egg
2 tablespoons milk
4 slices white toasting bread
**2 tablespoons Cinnamon Sugar
  (see page 99)**

Preheat Sandwich Toaster. Lightly beat the egg and milk together in a shallow dish. Quickly dip each side of 2 pieces of bread into egg mixture. Place in toaster and sprinkle each with 2 teaspoons of Cinnamon Sugar. Repeat dipping with remaining bread and place on top of the Cinnamon Sugar. Close toaster and cook for 1½-2 minutes. Dust sandwiches with the remaining Cinnamon Sugar before serving.

French Cinnamon Toasts

Serves 3-6

½ cup raisins
1 tablespoon rum
30 g butter or margarine
1 tablespoon honey
125 g cream cheese
6 slices bread, crusts removed and
    buttered on 1 side
1 tablespoon Cinnamon Sugar (see
    page 99)
whipped cream, optional

Soak raisins in rum for at least 15 minutes, then fry gently in butter or margarine until plump and crisp. Set aside. Beat honey with cream cheese until creamy, add cooled raisins. Preheat Sandwich Toaster. Divide mixture between bread slices. Place bread into preheated Sandwich Toaster, top with remaining bread, buttered sides up and cook for 2-3 minutes. Sprinkle with Cinnamon Sugar and serve hot with whipped cream.

Miss Diana Allen, Newlyn R.S.D., Vic. 3364.

Hawaiian Dream

Serves 4

125 g cottage cheese
¼ cup sugar
1 teaspoon lemon juice
pulp of 2 passionfruit
1 x 450-g can crushed pineapple,
    drained
1 banana, finely diced
8 slices bread, buttered on 1 side
mint leaves for garnish

Beat cottage cheese with sugar until smooth. Add lemon juice and passionfruit pulp and combine well. Fold pineapple and banana into mixture. Preheat Sandwich Toaster. Place 4 slices of bread, buttered sides down, in scallops. Divide the mixture between them, top with remaining slices, buttered sides up, and cook for 2 minutes or until golden brown. Serve garnished with fresh mint leaves.

Mrs M.J. Thomas, 5 Briar Court, Fulham Gardens, S.A. 5024.

Lost Bread

Serves 4

non-stick cooking spray or butter
2 x 60-g eggs
pinch salt
1½ tablespoons sugar
½ cup milk
2 tablespoons dry sherry
8 slices white bread
2 tablespoons Cinnamon Sugar
    (see page 99)
honey, optional

This is a marvellous way to use up very stale bread.
Preheat Sandwich Toaster and spray scallops with non-stick spray or brush with butter. Beat the eggs in a bowl with salt and sugar. Gradually beat in the milk and sherry. Dip 4 slices of bread into the egg mixture, quickly coating both sides. Place 2 pieces of dipped bread together and cook in Sandwich Toaster, 2 at a time, for 1½-2 minutes or until crisp and golden. Repeat with remaining bread slices. Serve hot sprinkled with Cinnamon Sugar and honey, if liked.

Sultana Nut Bread

Serves 4

8 slices white or fruit bread
butter
½ cup sultanas
4 tablespoons chopped walnuts
4 tablespoons honey
1 teaspoon mixed spices

Preheat Sandwich Toaster and butter bread on 1 side. Mix remaining ingredients thoroughly together. Place 2 slices of bread, buttered sides down, into toaster. Divide half the filling between the 2 scallops, top with 2 more slices of bread, buttered sides up. Close toaster and cook for 2 minutes or until golden. Repeat with remaining bread and filling. Serve hot or cold.

Turkish Fruit Delight
(Pictured on page 48)
Serves 4

2 rounds Lebanese flatbread
2 peaches, fresh or canned
1 tablespoon chopped almonds
1 tablespoon honey
3 tablespoons brandy
1 medium banana, sliced
30 g melted butter or margarine

Split Lebanese bread rounds into 4 halves. Chop or crush peaches and mix with almonds, honey, brandy and sliced banana. Let stand for 15 minutes. Divide mixture between 4 pieces of flatbread, fold sides of bread over fruit filling to form envelopes. Preheat Sandwich Toaster, brush each scallop with melted butter or margarine and cook Turkish Fruit Delights for 2-3 minutes. Serve hot or cold with cream, sour cream or ice cream.

Mrs M. Dulhunty, 55 Neutral Street, North Sydney, N.S.W. 2060.

Waffled sandwiches

1 tablespoon cream cheese, mixed with:

2 teaspoons sieved marmalade,
2 teaspoons currants,
1 teaspoon chopped nuts;
or
2 teaspoons grated orange rind,
6 stoned green olives, chopped;
or
2 tablespoons finely chopped ham,
1 teaspoon Dijon mustard.

1 hard-boiled egg, finely chopped, mixed with:

½ teaspoon curry powder,
1 tablespoon Cheddar cheese, grated
4 slices cucumber, chopped,
salt and pepper;
or
30 g ham, finely chopped,
2 teaspoons fruit chutney,
¼ teaspoon hot mustard;
or
2 sardines, drained and mashed,
2 shallots (spring onions), finely chopped.

1 tablespoon cooked, minced turkey, mixed with:

2 teaspoons cranberry jelly,
1 teaspoon chopped pine nuts, salt and pepper;
or
2 teaspoons mayonnaise,
1 tablespoon liverwurst or pâté;
or
2 shallots (spring onions), finely chopped,
2 teaspoons chopped mustard pickle.

1 tablespoon peanut butter, mixed with:

4 stoned dates, finely chopped,
2 teaspoons sieved marmalade;
or
1 tablespoon grated carrot,
1 tablespoon sultanas;
or
1 small mashed banana,
1 teaspoon fruit chutney;
or
1 tablespoon drained, crushed pineapple,
scant ¼ teaspoon ground cinnamon.

Trim crusts from bread, and butter 1 side of each slice. Choose white or brown milkbread of sandwich thickness, light rye or sourdough bread. Spread unbuttered sides of bread with any of the complementary sandwich fillings listed. Top with remaining bread slices and cook in preheated Wafflemaker for 2 minutes. The quantities given are for 2 sandwiches.
Note: Do not use bread of toasting thickness.

Savoury rolls

Savoury rolls, using a variety of breads, may be served in many ways. Delicious as party food and hors d'oeuvre, a fun snack or accompaniment to soup, they may be prepared well in advance and cooked when you are ready.

Trim crusts from bread, brush with melted butter, or for added interest use one of the Flavoured Butters on page 100, then place filling on the bread and roll up diagonally. Secure with short pieces of cocktail sticks and cook for approximately 2 minutes. Ensure that the filling is not too runny and irrespective of which Sandwich Toaster you are using, always lay the rolls parallel to the cutters.

It is also possible to use some of these fillings in mini sandwiches and pastry puffs.

Garlic Rolls

Makes 12

12 slices bread
1 quantity Garlic Butter (see page 100), melted

Preheat Sandwich Toaster. Brush both sides of trimmed bread with Garlic Butter, roll diagonally and secure with cocktail sticks. Cook for 2 minutes and serve whole or sliced with soup, or the main meal.

Prosciutto and Melon Rolls

Serves 6-8

6-8 slices bread
2 tablespoons melted butter
6-8 slices prosciutto ham
½ rock-melon, de-seeded and cut into strips, 1-cm square
freshly ground black pepper

Preheat Sandwich Toaster. Brush 1 side of bread with melted butter. Lay a slice of prosciutto onto unbuttered side of each slice of bread. Place a melon strip across the ham and season generously with freshly ground black pepper. Roll bread diagonally and secure with cocktail sticks. Cook rolls for 1½-2 minutes or until crisp. Serve hot or cold.

Beef and Horseradish Rolls

Makes 6

½ cup minced cold roast beef
2 tablespoons horseradish relish
salt and freshly ground black pepper
6 slices bread
2 tablespoons melted butter

Combine minced beef, horseradish and season to taste with salt and freshly ground black pepper. Preheat Sandwich Toaster. Brush 1 side of bread with melted butter. Spread filling onto unbuttered sides of bread, roll diagonally, secure with cocktail sticks and cook for 2 minutes.
Variation: Omit horseradish and spread bread liberally with mustard. Sprinkle minced beef over bread, roll and cook as above.

Smoked Oyster Rolls

Makes 8-10

**8-10 slices wholemeal milk or white
   bread
4 tablespoons melted butter
1 x 100-g can smoked oysters,
   drained
2 teaspoons lemon juice
cayenne pepper for sprinkling**

Preheat Sandwich Toaster. Brush 1 side of bread slices with melted butter. Halve oysters if large and lay in a row across 1 corner of the unbuttered sides of bread. Sprinkle oysters lightly with a few drops of lemon juice and cayenne pepper. Roll up, secure with cocktail sticks and cook for 2 minutes.
Variation: Spread bread slices with Lemon Butter (see page 100) before adding oysters. Omit lemon juice and sprinkle with cayenne before rolling. Smoked mussels can also be used in the same way.

Swedish Smoked Salmon Rolls

Makes 8-10

**8-10 slices light rye or white bread
2-3 tablespoons melted butter
125 g smoked salmon, chopped
60 g cream cheese
1 teaspoon lemon juice
2 teaspoons sour cream
salt and pepper to taste
2 tablespoons fresh dill, finely
   chopped or 1 teaspoon dried dill**

These are delicious for a special occasion or make them just to spoil yourself.
Preheat Sandwich Toaster. Brush trimmed bread with melted butter on 1 side. Thoroughly combine smoked salmon, cheese, lemon juice and sour cream. Season to taste with salt and pepper. Spread mixture onto unbuttered sides of bread and sprinkle lightly with dill. Roll up diagonally, secure with cocktail sticks and cook for 2 minutes. Cut each roll in half and serve piping hot.

Sardine Pâté Rolls

Makes 14

**2 x 105-g cans sardines, drained
4 hard-boiled eggs, chopped
½ cup finely minced or chopped
   onion
1-2 tablespoons mayonnaise
1 teaspoon Dijon mustard
3-4 teaspoons lemon juice
14 slices rye or wholemeal bread
4 tablespoons melted butter**

Split sardines and remove backbones. In a bowl mash sardines well and blend in finely chopped eggs, minced onion, half of the mayonnaise, mustard and lemon juice. Add remaining mayonnaise if the mixture is too stiff. Chill. When ready to cook preheat Sandwich Toaster. Brush 1 side of bread with melted butter. Spread pâté on unbuttered sides of bread. Roll diagonally, secure with cocktail sticks and cook for 2 minutes. Serve hot or cold with a side dish of midget dill pickles.

Tuna Nut Rolls

Makes 12-14

**12-14 slices wholemeal bread
3 tablespoons melted butter
1 x 185-g can tuna, drained
½ cup finely chopped parsley
½ cup very finely chopped celery
½ cup chopped walnuts
1-2 tablespoons mayonnaise**

Preheat Sandwich Toaster. Brush trimmed bread with melted butter on 1 side. Combine all ingredients using just enough mayonnaise to bind. Spread filling on unbuttered sides of bread, and roll up diagonally. Secure with cocktail sticks and cook for 2 minutes.

Turkey Delight Rolls

Makes 10-12

10-12 slices bread
1 quantity Parsley Butter (see page 101 or 4 tablespoons melted butter
1 cup finely diced cooked turkey meat
1-2 tablespoons mayonnaise
1 teaspoon curry powder or to taste
60 g salted almonds, roughly chopped

This is a lovely way to use up the last remnants of turkey, particularly the dark meat.
Preheat Sandwich Toaster. Spread bread slices with Parsley Butter or brush with melted butter. Combine turkey meat with mayonnaise and curry powder to taste. Add chopped almonds and a little more of the mayonnaise if the mixture is too dry. Place a layer of the mixture across corner of unbuttered side of each slice of bread. Roll up and secure with cocktail sticks. Cook for 2 minutes. Serve hot or cold.
Note: If these are to be served cold use a little more curry powder as cold food loses some of its flavour.
Variation: If curry flavour is not your favourite, try replacing the curry powder with 2 teaspoons fresh tarragon or a generous half teaspoon of dried tarragon.

Kippered Cheese Rolls

Makes 14

14 slices milk bread
4 tablespoons melted butter or ½ quantity Lemon Butter (see page 100)
1 x 200-g can kipper fillets, drained
125 g cream cheese
2 teaspoons lemon juice or 2 teaspoons white vinegar
1 tablespoon finely chopped chives
¼ teaspoon cayenne pepper
1 tablespoon finely chopped parsley

Spread 1 side of bread slices with Lemon Butter or brush with melted butter. Mash kipper fillets and combine thoroughly with cream cheese. Omit lemon juice or vinegar if Lemon Butter has been used, otherwise add lemon juice to kippers with chives, cayenne pepper and parsley. Preheat Sandwich Toaster. Spread kipper mixture onto unbuttered sides of bread slices, roll and secure. Cook for 2 minutes and serve piping hot.

This method of making Apple Charlotte (see page 38) is quick and the results are delicious. Use attractive fruit and nut bread and cook Apple Charlotte in an Electric Jaffle to make a dessert or use a Snackmaker or Sandwich Toaster to make smaller shapes.

Overleaf: A feast of appealing flavours and shapes, all cooked with a minimum of fuss. The large plate on the left page shows crisp pastry delights, mini pieces of Baklava (see page 63) which is a traditional Greek sweet using nuts and syrup, and Turkish Fruit Delight (see page 42) which contains peaches, bananas, honey, nuts and brandy and is made from Lebanese flatbread.
At the back, Greek Spinach Pies (see page 58) are made in an Electric Jaffle. The right page shows delectable Chocolate Eclairs (see page 61) made with Choux Pastry and filled with whipped cream. At right, perfect luncheon dishes, Vegetable Pies (see page 59) made with Herb Shortcrust Pastry and cooked in an Electric Jaffle. At the back, delicious Seafood Quiche (see page 60) which can be made using any of the sandwich-toasting appliances.

Cheese and Beer Rolls

Makes 14-16

2 cups grated Cheddar cheese
½ cup softened butter
¼ cup beer
1 teaspoon tabasco sauce
1 teaspoon Worcestershire sauce
14-16 slices wholemeal bread,
 trimmed
¼ cup melted butter

Preheat Sandwich Toaster. Combine grated cheese with softened butter. Add enough beer to bind and season with tabasco and Worcestershire sauces. Brush 1 side of bread with melted butter, spread unbuttered sides with filling, roll and secure with cocktail sticks. Cook for 2 minutes or until crisp and golden.
Note: These rolls are delicious alone or with Onion Soup (see page 89).

Date and Cheddar Cheese Rolls

Makes 10

20 dates, pitted
½ cup strong Cheddar cheese
1 tablespoon brandy
10 slices bread
½ quantity Lemon Butter (see page 100)

Chop dates finely. Cut Cheddar cheese into small dice, combine with dates and add brandy. Set aside and allow to marinate until most of the brandy has been absorbed. Preheat Sandwich Toaster. Spread both sides of bread thinly with Lemon Butter. Lay a row of filling across 1 corner of bread slices. Roll securely and fasten with cocktail sticks. Cook for 2 minutes.

Devilled Egg and Sesame Seed Rolls

Serves 4-6

2 tablespoons sesame seeds,
 toasted
2 hard-boiled eggs, chopped
½ cup finely chopped celery
2-3 tablespoons mayonnaise
1 teaspoon Dijon mustard
2 tablespoons finely chopped
 shallots (spring onions)
4-6 slices bread

Combine all ingredients using only enough mayonnaise to bind. Chill. When ready to use, preheat Sandwich Toaster. Butter bread on 1 side only and spread filling on unbuttered sides. Roll up and secure with cocktail sticks. Cook for 2 minutes or until crisp and golden.
Note: Sesame seeds can be toasted in a shallow pan for 6-7 minutes. Place seeds in pan and shake occasionally until the seeds are evenly browned. Use them to sprinkle on Waffled Sandwiches (see page 43) or in salads.

Asparagus Rolls
(Pictured opposite)

½ cup butter, melted
1 slice bread for each asparagus
 spear
1 x 340-g can asparagus spears,
 drained

Preheat Sandwich Toaster. Brush trimmed slices of bread with melted butter on 1 side only. Place 1 piece of asparagus on a corner of the unbuttered sides of bread and roll up diagonally. Secure with cocktail sticks and cook for 2 minutes.
Variation: Spread unbuttered sides of bread lightly with cream cheese before rolling.

*Perfect for a late supper, Asparagus Rolls (see above)
are a good accompaniment to Carrot Soup (see page 88).
Cook the rolls in a Snackmaker and turn them in the scallops
during the cooking time to achieve an attractive pattern.*

Using pastry

To extend the use of your sandwich-toasting appliance, enclose sweet or savoury fillings in pastry. Make one of the pastry recipes here or used the frozen variety. Also spring rolls or filo pastry delights may be cooked quickly, economically and with tasty results. Cut selected pastry to fit the scallops of your appliance, allowing about 5 mm extra to make room for the filling. For the 4-Up and 8-Up Snackmakers and Snack 'n' Sandwich Toasters cut pastry 12.5 cm square; for an Electric Jaffle, 11.5 cm square. Brush pastry with melted butter, oil or margarine and place squares, buttered sides down onto lower scallops of the preheated appliance. Add filling level with tops of scallops, cover with pastry, buttered sides up and cook without clamping until crisp and golden. Trim any excess pastry with a sharp knife.

Puff Pastry

250 g butter
2 cups plain flour
pinch salt
1 egg yolk
2 teaspoons lemon juice
½-⅔ cup cold water

Shape butter into a rectangle approximately 2.5 cm thick, cool in refrigerator. Sift flour and salt together. Beat the egg yolk lightly with the lemon juice and half a cup of water. Add water mixture to the flour, mixing until well combined. Add enough of the remaining water to the mixture to form a soft, but not sticky dough. Turn dough onto a lightly floured board and knead well. Roll to a thickness of 1 cm. Place cooled butter onto half of the rolled pastry, fold pastry over the butter and seal it inside the pastry by pressing firmly with rolling pin. Turn the pastry until the fold is at the right-hand side. Roll the pastry into a thin sheet, rolling away from you at all times. Fold pastry into 3 and set aside in the refrigerator to rest for 10 minutes. Repeat rolling and folding twice, allow to rest again for 10 minutes before using as required.
Note: This pastry freezes well.

Filo Pastry

This fine pastry is available from most delicatessens and supermarkets. It may be used for a variety of sweet and savoury dishes. As the pastry is so fine it dries out quickly so cover it with a damp cloth after removing from the packet. To use filo in a Sandwich Toaster brush 1 side of each sheet with melted butter and press layers of 4 squares into each scallop. Top with layers of 4 squares.

Choux Pastry

60 g butter
1¼ cups water
1 cup plain flour, sifted
3 x 60-g eggs

Choux Pastry is very simple to make and needs no rolling or resting time. It can be used in a variety of ways with savoury or sweet fillings.

Place the butter and water into a saucepan and simmer gently until the butter has melted. Remove pan from the heat and tip all of the flour into the liquid. Stir ingredients together until a smooth paste forms. Return mixture to the heat and cook, stirring constantly until the mixture leaves the sides of the saucepan clean and forms a ball round the spoon. Allow mixture to cool slightly for 3-4 minutes. Add the eggs, 1 at a time, beating well after each addition. Use as required.

Choux Pastry Cooking Times

	Electric Jaffle	4-Up & 8-Up Snackmaker	Snack 'n' Sandwich Toaster
Small choux puffs, unfilled, 1 level tablespoon mixture	2 per scallop 8 - 10 minutes	1 per scallop 7 - 8 minutes	1 per scallop 7 - 8 minutes
Sandwich-sized choux puffs, unfilled, 2 level tablespoons	2 per scallop 8 - 10 minutes	1 per scallop 7 - 8 minutes	1 per scallop 7 - 8 minutes
Sandwich-sized choux puffs with filling	1 per scallop 10 - 12 minutes	Not Suitable	1 per scallop 8 - 10 minutes

Cheese Pastry

1¼ cups flour
½ teaspoon salt
¼ teaspoon cayenne pepper
125 g Cheddar cheese, grated finely
125 g butter, softened
cold water if necessary

Sift flour with salt and cayenne. Mix in the grated cheese. Rub the butter into the flour mixture using your fingertips. Work well together; the mixture should combine into a dry dough without the addition of any water. This depends a little on the condition of the cheese. If necessary add only enough water to form a very dry dough. Chill pastry for 20 minutes before using.

Shortcrust Pastry

½ cup plain flour
½ cup self-raising flour
¼ teaspoon salt
60 g butter or margarine
1 egg yolk
enough iced water to mix

Sift flour and salt together. Rub the butter or margarine into the flour with the tips of the fingers until the mixture resembles breadcrumbs. Add the egg yolk and only enough water to form a dry dough. Set pastry aside to rest for a while before rolling thinly, to about 3 mm thick.
Note: Pastry should be handled as little as possible for best results. Try to have everything cold and work very quickly.
Variations: Sweet Shortcrust Pastry. Add 2 teaspoons sugar to dry ingredients before rubbing in butter.
Herb Pastry. Add half a teaspoon of mixed dried herbs and 4 parsley sprigs, finely chopped, to dry ingredients.

Savoury pies and puffs

Cheesy Onion Pies

Makes 4-6

30 g butter
250 g onions, finely sliced
salt and freshly ground black
  pepper
1 egg, lightly beaten
1 tablespoon cream
1 tablespoon grated Parmesan
  cheese
1 quantity Cheese Pastry
  (see page 53)
melted butter for brushing

Melt butter in a shallow pan, add onions and fry gently until they are golden in colour but not browned. Season with a little salt and lashings of freshly ground black pepper. Remove pan from heat, stir egg into hot onion mixture and combine well. Add cream and Parmesan and mix together thoroughly. Preheat Sandwich Toaster or Snackmaker. Roll Cheese Pastry thinly, cut to size required for your appliance. Lightly brush 1 side of pastry pieces with melted butter and place them butter sides down, in the scallops. Fill scallops level with top, cover with remaining pastry, buttered sides up, and cook for 4-5 minutes or until golden in colour. Serve hot with broccoli or other green vegetable in season or cold with salad.

Cheese Surprise

Makes 4-6

1 quantity Cheese Pastry
  (see page 53)
melted butter or margarine for
  brushing
1 tablespoon clear marmalade
1 cup finely shredded lettuce
½ cup sultanas
½ cup slivered or coarsely
  chopped nuts

This mixture of fruit, lettuce and nuts has a lovely texture and the flavours combine well together.
Roll pastry to about 3-mm thickness and cut to size. Preheat Sandwich Toaster. Brush 1 side of each piece lightly with butter or margarine and press, buttered sides down, into scallops. Combine filling ingredients together and fill scallops before topping with remaining pastry, buttered sides up. Cook for 4-5 minutes. Serve hot or cold.

Ham and Cheese Puffs

Makes 12-14

125 g ham, minced or finely diced
2 tablespoons grated Parmesan
  cheese
1 x 60-g egg, lightly beaten
¾ cup cream
salt and pepper to taste
pinch nutmeg
1 quantity Choux Pastry
  (see page 53)
vegetable oil for brushing

These filled puffs rise considerably so they should only be made in the Electric Jaffle.
Place ham, cheese and egg into a bowl and mix well. Heat cream in a small pan until just bubbling, pour over the ham mixture and stir all ingredients together until thoroughly combined. Season to taste with salt, pepper and nutmeg. Set aside.
Make Choux Pastry and preheat Electric Jaffle. Lightly oil the scallops. Spread 1 generous tablespoon Choux in each scallop. Place 1 level tablespoon of filling onto pastry and top with 2 teaspoons of Choux. Cook for time given in table on page 53. Repeat until all ingredients are used. Serve hot or cold.

Tyropokita
Greek Feta Cheese Puffs

Serves 4

1 quantity Puff Pastry (see page 52), or 1 x 375-g packet frozen puff pastry or filo pastry
melted butter for brushing
125 g feta cheese
2 tablespoons lemon juice
1 small onion, minced
1 clove garlic, crushed
1 tablespoon finely chopped mint or ¼ teaspoon dried mint
½ teaspoon oregano
2 large leaves silver beet or spinach, very finely chopped
2 tablespoons chopped parsley
1 egg yolk
pinch ground cinnamon

Roll out puff pastry thinly and cut to size, allowing 5 mm extra on edges. Brush 1 side lightly with melted butter or margarine. Preheat Sandwich Toaster and press pastry, buttered sides down, into scallops. Combine remaining ingredients in a bowl and fill pastry pieces level with top of scallops. Top with remaining pastry, buttered sides up, and cook for 3-4 minutes. Serve with Tomato Anchovy Salad (see page 92).

Kouliabiaka
Swedish Salmon Puffs

Serves 4

15 g butter
1 small onion, finely chopped
125 g mushrooms, finely sliced
1 x 220-g can red salmon, drained
½ cup cooked rice
2 tablespoons chopped parsley
salt and pepper to taste
1 quantity Puff Pastry (see page 52) or 1 packet frozen puff pastry
vegetable oil for brushing
2 hard-boiled eggs, sliced

Heat the butter and lightly fry the onion until just transparent. Add mushrooms and cook for 1 minute. Cool mixture. Add onion mixture to flaked salmon, rice and parsley. Mix together and season to taste with salt and pepper. Roll pastry thinly, allowing an extra 5 mm over the scallop size. Oil pastry lightly. Preheat Sandwich Toaster and lay cut pastry, oiled sides down, into the scallops. Spoon enough of the salmon mixture into each pie to bring it level with the top of the scallop, lay egg slices onto filling and cover with remaining pastry, oiled sides up. Close lid and cook for 4-5 minutes.
Note: Make Kouliabiaka into mini puffs and serve as delicious appetisers. Turn the puffs across the cutters halfway through the cooking time.

Sweet and Sour Prawn Puffs
(Pictured on half title page at front of book)
Serves 4

125 g school prawns, peeled
1 stalk celery, sliced
½ red capsicum, chopped
1 shallot (spring onion), sliced
2 tablespoons sweet and sour sauce, bottled or home-made
salt and pepper
1 quantity Puff Pastry (see page 52) or 1 packet frozen puff pastry

Combine all filling ingredients. Preheat Sandwich Toaster. Cut Puff Pastry to fit scallops and brush 1 side of each sheet lightly with melted butter. Place pastry buttered sides down onto scallops, and spoon enough filling onto each piece to come level with the top of the scallops. Top with remaining pastry, buttered sides up. Lower lid and cook until pastry is golden brown.

Fish Pie

Serves 4

60 g butter, melted
2 pieces preserved ginger, drained
and finely chopped
1 tablespoon seedless raisins
1 tablespoon chopped, blanched
almonds
500 g cooked fish, fresh or canned
and flaked
1 quantity Puff Pastry (see page 52)
or 1 packet of frozen puff pastry

This is a piquant sweet-savoury pie. The best result is obtained when made in the Electric Jaffle. Serve it with Herb Sauce on page 99.
Mix together melted butter, ginger, raisins and nuts. Roll pastry thinly and cut pieces to size. Oil lightly on 1 side. Preheat Sandwich Toaster. Lay pastry oiled sides down onto a flat surface and spread 1 teaspoon of ginger mixture over each of 4 pieces. Divide flaked fish between the pies and cover fish with remaining ginger mixture. Top with pastry, oiled sides up, and cook for 5 minutes or until puffed and golden. Serve the pies with a vegetable and hot Herb Sauce or cold with a crisp salad. This goes very well with Cucumber Salad on page 90.
Note: As the fish is already cooked it probably does not need further seasoning but this can be adjusted if necessary. Any fish can be used.

Tuna Curry Pies

Makes 4-6

1 x 185-g can tuna and onion,
drained
60 g cream cheese
2 teaspoons curry powder, or to
taste
salt
1 clove garlic, crushed
2 teaspoons lemon juice
1 small egg
1 quantity Shortcrust Pastry (see
page 53), or 1 packet frozen
shortcrust pastry

Mash tuna with cream cheese and mix well with the curry powder. Season with salt if necessary. Mix crushed garlic with the lemon juice and beat into the tuna mixture with the egg. Roll pastry thinly, cut to size and oil lightly on 1 side. Preheat Sandwich Toaster. Press pastry, oiled sides down, into scallops. Fill scallops just a little more than level with the scallop tops, cover with remaining pastry, oiled sides up, and cook for 4-6 minutes. Serve hot with new potatoes and crisp green vegetables.
Variation: Make your own or use frozen puff pastry and the above filling for Tuna Curry Puffs.

Veal, Ham and Egg Pies

Serves 4

1 quantity Shortcrust Pastry or
Puff Pastry (see pages 52 or 53)
or 1 packet frozen pastry,
thawed
melted butter for brushing
3 eggs, lightly beaten
½ cup cream
125 g cooked veal, diced
90 g leg ham, diced
salt and pepper to taste
1 hard-boiled egg, sliced

Roll pastry to a thickness of 3 mm. Cut to fit scallops and brush 1 side of each pastry piece lightly with melted butter. Preheat Sandwich Toaster. Combine eggs and cream. Add diced meats and season to taste with salt and pepper. Lay pastry into scallops, buttered sides down. Spoon enough of the filling into each pastry base to come level with the top of the scallops. Top filling with 2 slices of hard-boiled egg and cover with remaining pastry, buttered sides up. Close lid and cook for 4-5 minutes. Serve hot or cold with salad or vegetables.

Creamed Veal Pies

Serves 4

15 g butter
60 g mushrooms, chopped
1 tablespoon flour
¼ cup milk
1 chicken stock cube
1 tablespoon finely chopped
   parsley
1 teaspoon lemon juice
250 g cooked veal, minced or finely
   chopped
salt and pepper to taste
1 quantity Shortcrust Pastry (see
   page 53), or 1 packet frozen
   shortcrust pastry
melted butter for brushing
60 g Cheddar cheese, grated

A little bit of pre-cooking is involved to make these pies but they are worth the effort.
Melt butter and gently cook the chopped mushrooms for 1 minute. Sprinkle with flour and stir until the flour is absorbed by the butter. Add the milk, stirring constantly until a thick sauce is formed. The sauce should be thick but if it is too gluggy add a little more milk 1 teaspoonful at a time. Crumble the chicken stock cube into the sauce and cook gently for another minute. Stir in the parsley and lemon juice with the minced meat and season to taste with salt and pepper. Cool.
Preheat Sandwich Toaster. Roll pastry thinly to 3 mm and cut to fit scallops. Brush melted butter lightly on 1 side of each piece. Lay pastry into scallops, buttered sides down, and spoon enough of the filling into each to come level with the top of each scallop. Divide cheese into 4 and sprinkle over the filling of each pie. Top with remaining pastry, buttered sides up, close toaster and cook for 4-5 minutes or until pastry is crisp and golden. Serve hot with vegetables or a crisp salad.
Variation: Creamed Lamb Pie. Substitute 250 g cooked lamb for the veal.

Paprika Veal

Serves 4

1 quantity Shortcrust Pastry (see
   page 53) or 1 packet frozen
   shortcrust pastry or 8 slices
   white bread
melted butter for brushing
2 tablespoons tomato paste
2 tablespoons sour cream or 2
   tablespoons cream mixed with 1
   teaspoon lemon juice
1 teaspoon paprika pepper
185 g cooked veal, minced or finely
   diced
1 medium onion, finely sliced and
   separated into rings
salt and pepper to taste

Here is another way to use leftover veal or lamb. Paprika Veal is delicious in pies or sandwiches.
Roll pastry to a thickness of 3 mm and cut to fit scallops. Lightly brush melted butter on 1 side of each piece or each bread slice. Preheat Sandwich Toaster. Combine tomato paste with sour cream or cream and lemon juice. Mix paprika into the cream mixture. Spread unbuttered sides of bread or pastry pieces with paprika paste. Divide minced veal between 4 portions of bread or pastry, top with onion rings and season with salt and pepper. Cover with remaining pastry or bread, buttered sides up, and place into toaster. Close and cook sandwiches for 2 minutes, pastry for 4-5 minutes. Serve hot with vegetables of choice.
Variation: Paprika Lamb. Substitute 185 g cooked lamb for veal.

Corned Beef Pasties

Makes 4-6

30 g butter or margarine
2 onions, finely chopped
1 x 340-g can corned beef
2 hard-boiled eggs, chopped
salt and pepper to taste
1-2 tablespoons cream
1 quantity Shortcrust Pastry (see
    page 53), or 1 packet frozen
    shortcrust pastry
vegetable oil for brushing

Heat the butter and fry onions lightly until just softened. Set aside. Mash the corned beef and mix with the onions. Add the hard-boiled eggs and combine well. Season to taste with salt and pepper and add cream if the mixture seems too stiff. Preheat Sandwich Toaster and lightly oil the scallops. Roll pastry thinly, cut to size and press into scallops. Add enough filling to come just above the top of the scallops. Cover with remaining pastry and cook for 4-6 minutes. Serve hot or cold.
Note: You may prefer them cold with salad or alone with a little mustard.

Creamed Chicken Pies

Serves 4

15 g butter
1 tablespoon flour
100 ml milk
250 g cooked chicken, diced
1 hard-boiled egg, chopped
1 tablespoon chopped chives
1 tablespoon finely chopped
    parsley
2-3 tablespoons cream
salt and pepper to taste
1 quantity Shortcrust or Puff
    Pastry (see pages 52 or 53) or 1
    packet frozen pastry
melted butter for brushing

Any of the pastry recipes can be used for this pie; Shortcrust and Puff are particularly good.
Melt butter in a pan, add the flour and mix well. Cook gently for 1 minute. Add the milk gradually, stirring between each addition until a smooth sauce is formed. The sauce should be quite thick. Stir the chicken, egg, chives and parsley into the sauce with enough cream to thin the sauce without making it too runny. Season to taste with salt and pepper. Set aside to cool.
Preheat Sandwich Toaster. Roll pastry to a thickness of 3-4 mm. Cut to fit scallops. Lightly brush 1 side of each piece with melted butter. Line scallops with pastry and spoon enough of the filling into each pie to come just level with the top of the scallop. Top with remaining pastry, buttered sides up, close toaster and cook for 4-6 minutes or until pastry is crisp and golden. Serve hot or cold.
Note: If these pies are served cold, ensure that there is plenty of seasoning.

Greek Spinach Pies

(Pictured on page 48)
Serves 4-6

1 bunch spinach (silver beet),
    cooked, drained and finely
    chopped
6 shallots (spring onions), cut into
    5-mm rings
125 g feta cheese, grated
125 g mozzarella cheese, grated
3 eggs, lightly beaten
¼ teaspoon dried dill
salt and pepper to taste
1 x 375-g packet filo pastry
⅓ cup melted butter for brushing

Combine all the filling ingredients together and set aside. Preheat Sandwich Toaster. Brush each sheet of pastry lightly with butter. Do this in groups of 4 so that you have pastry sheets of 4 thicknesses for the base and top of the pies. Cut the buttered pastry to fit scallops and lay buttered sides down. Spoon enough filling onto the pastry to bring it level with the top of each scallop. Cover with the next 4 sheets of pastry, buttered sides up. Close toaster and cook for 3-4 minutes or until pastry is crisp and golden brown.
Note: Turn pies halfway through cooking time to make appealing mini pies.

Vegetable Pies

(Pictured on page 49)
Serves 4

12 shallots (spring onions), cut into
    5-mm rings, including green tops
2 tomatoes, peeled and thinly
    sliced
250 g potatoes, cooked and sliced
60 g Cheddar cheese, grated
4 tablespoons cream
salt and pepper to taste
1 quantity Shortcrust, Herb or
    Cheese Pastry (see page 53)
    or 1 packet frozen shortcrust
    pastry
oil or melted butter for brushing

These Vegetable Pies may be served as a lunch dish on their own, perhaps with a crisp salad, or as an accompaniment to hot or cold meat.
Divide shallots, tomatoes and potatoes into 4. Mix cheese with cream and set aside. Preheat Sandwich Toaster. Roll pastry to a thickness of 3 mm, and cut to fit scallops. Lightly oil or butter 1 side of each piece. Lay a piece of pastry, greased sides down, into each scallop and cover pastry with shallots, tomatoes and potatoes. Sprinkle with salt and pepper. Spoon a quarter of the cream mixture over each vegetable filling, cover with remaining pastry, greased sides up. Close toaster and cook for 4-5 minutes or until pastry is crisp and golden. Serve hot.

Mushroom Turnovers

Makes 10-12

500 g mushrooms, chopped
45 g butter or margarine
2 tablespoons flour
¾-1 cup cream
salt and pepper to taste
1 quantity Shortcrust Pastry (see
    page 53) or 1 packet frozen
    shortcrust pastry
oil or melted butter for brushing

Add mushrooms to butter in a shallow pan and cook over a gentle heat for 8-10 minutes. Sprinkle mushrooms with flour and stir well. Gradually add enough cream, stirring constantly, until mixture has thickened. The mixture should not be too runny. Cool. Season to taste with salt and pepper.
Preheat Sandwich Toaster. Roll pastry to 3-mm thickness and cut to size. Lightly oil or butter 1 side of each piece. Lay pastry, greased sides down, into scallops of toaster. Fill scallops level with tops and lay remaining pastry over, greased sides up. Lower cover and cook for 4-6 minutes or until crisp and golden.
Note: These are delicious served hot or cold and go very well with steak and a crisp salad.
Variation: 1 tablespoon dry sherry can be added to the mixture if liked.

Savoury Raisin Pies

Serves 4

1 quantity Shortcrust Pastry (see
    page 53) or 1 packet frozen
    shortcrust pastry
60 g ham, finely chopped
60 g Cheddar cheese, grated
2 tablespoons cream
1 x 60-g egg, lightly beaten
60 g seedless raisins
salt and pepper to taste

Roll pastry thinly to about 3 mm and cut to desired size for your Sandwich Toaster. Preheat toaster. Lightly butter 1 side of each piece of pastry. Lay pastry pieces, buttered sides down, in scallops. Mix all the filling ingredients together thoroughly and spoon enough of the filling onto the pastry-lined scallops to bring filling level with the scallop tops. Cover with remaining pastry, buttered sides up, and cook for 4 minutes or until crisp and golden. serve hot or cold.
Note: This filling can also be used in bread. Made into mini sandwiches or pies, the savoury raisin filling makes an unusual appetiser or snack.

Quiches

Individual quiches are another favourite which adapt readily to cooking in a Sandwich Toaster, Snackmaker or an Electric Jaffle. Marvellous for lunches at school or home, for picnics or outdoor entertaining on hot nights, quiches add variety to the weekly menu.

When using an Electric Jaffle more filling may be required. Use 2 small eggs and ½ cup of cream in the following recipes.

Quiche

Serves 4-6

1 quantity Shortcrust Pastry (see page 53) or 1 packet frozen shortcrust pastry
melted butter for brushing
1 x 60-g egg, lightly beaten
⅓ cup cream
¼ cup grated Cheddar cheese
4 shallots (spring onions), cut into 5-mm rings
salt and pepper to taste
pinch nutmeg

Roll pastry to a thickness of 3 mm and cut to fit scallops. Brush 1 side of each pastry square lightly with melted butter. Preheat Sandwich Toaster. Combine all the filling ingredients.

Lay a pastry square, buttered side down, into each scallop. Spoon enough of the filling mixture onto the pastry to come level with the top of each scallop. Top with remaining pastry, buttered sides up. Close lid and cook for 4-5 minutes. Serve hot or cold with a crisp salad.

Variations: Asparagus Quiche. To basic quiche filling add 2 tablespoons canned asparagus tips which have been well drained.

Tomato Quiche. To basic filling add 1 large tomato, which has been peeled, seeded and diced.

Ham Quiche. Add 2 tablespoons of diced ham to basic filling.

Seafood Quiche

(Pictured on page 49)
Serves 4

1 quantity Shortcrust Pastry (see page 53) or 1 packet frozen shortcrust pastry
melted butter for brushing
1 x 60-g egg, lightly beaten
⅓ cup cream
¼ cup grated gruyère cheese
1 tablespoon finely chopped parsley
2 shallots (spring onions), cut into 5-mm rings (reserve a few finely cut rings for garnish)
pinch garlic salt
90 g cooked prawns or scallops, diced
salt and pepper to taste

Roll pastry to a thickness of 3 mm. Cut to fit scallops and brush 1 side of each pastry square lightly with melted butter. Preheat Sandwich Toaster. Mix all the filling ingredients together and set aside.

Lay a pastry square, buttered side down, into each scallop. Spoon enough of the filling mixture onto the pastry to come level with the top of the scallops. Cover with remaining pastry, buttered sides up. Close lid and cook for 4-5 minutes. Serve hot with a salad and Lemony Brussels Sprouts (see page 93).

Dessert pies and puffs

Individual pies for desserts are very easy to make in a Sandwich Toaster, Snackmaker or an Electric Jaffle and the recipes in this section are just an indication of the variety. Choose a pastry, roll it to a thickness of about 3 mm and cut it to fit the scallops. Allow a little extra over the scallop size to accommodate the filling.

Chocolate Eclairs
(Pictured on page 49)

**1 quantity Choux Pastry
(see page 53)
non-stick cooking spray
1 cup cream, whipped
1 teaspoon vanilla essence**

Icing

**125 g cooking chocolate
4 tablespoons water
1½-2 cups icing sugar**

Make Choux Pastry and fill into an icing bag fitted with a large vegetable nozzle. Spray scallops with non-stick cooking spray and preheat Sandwich Toaster. Whip cream with the vanilla essence and set aside. Pipe fingers of Choux Pastry into scallops, lower lid and cook for times given in table on page 53. When fingers are cooked, cool. Split and pipe whipped cream into centres. Ice the tops with Chocolate Icing.

Icing
Melt the chocolate with the water, preferably in the top of a double boiler, or in a basin standing over hot water. When the chocolate has melted stir in only enough of the icing sugar to make a consistency thin enough to spread.

Custard Puffs

**1 quantity Choux Pastry
(see page 53)
1½ tablespoons cornflour
1 cup milk
1 egg, lightly beaten
½ teaspoon vanilla essence
1 tablespoon sugar**

This recipe is suitable for the Electric Jaffle only as the puffs rise too high to be made in the Sandwich Toasters. Make Choux Pastry. Preheat Electric Jaffle. Mix cornflour gradually with the milk until smooth. Pour into a saucepan with the egg, vanilla essence and sugar. Cook over a moderate heat, stirring constantly until custard thickens. Cook for 2 minutes. Spread 1 heaped tablespoon Choux Pastry into Electric Jaffle. Place 1 tablespoon custard onto Choux and top custard with 2 teaspoons of Choux Pastry. Close and cook according to cooking times on page 53.
Variation: For a richer filling, make custard with three-quarters cup of milk. When custard is cooked, cool slightly and beat in half a cup of whipped cream.

Fruit Mince Pies

**1 quantity Shortcrust Pastry (see page 53) or 1 packet frozen shortcrust pastry
melted butter for brushing
1 x 425-g jar fruit mince
icing sugar for dusting, optional**

Preheat Sandwich Toaster. Roll pastry to a thickness of 3 mm and cut to fit scallops. Brush melted butter lightly on 1 side of pastry pieces. Lay pastry squares, buttered sides down, into scallops. Spoon 2 teaspoons of the fruit mince into the scallops, cover with remaining pastry, buttered sides up, close lid and cook for 3-4 minutes.
Variation: Place 3 or 4 thin slices of apple into each scallop before adding the mince.

Pumpkin Pie

Serves 4-6

1 quantity Shortcrust Pastry (see page 53) or 1 packet frozen shortcrust pastry
melted butter for brushing
1 cup cooked, mashed pumpkin
½ cup brown sugar, or to taste
pinch salt
½ teaspoon cinnamon
½ teaspoon nutmeg
¼ teaspoon ground ginger
pinch ground cloves
1 egg, beaten
2 tablespoons cream
whipped cream or ice cream for serving

Roll pastry to a thickness of 3 mm and cut to fit scallops. Lightly brush 1 side of each pastry piece with melted butter. Preheat Sandwich Toaster. Combine ingredients in the order given. Lay pastry pieces into scallops. Spoon enough of the pumpkin mixture into each scallop to bring it barely above the level of the scallop. Top with remaining pastry buttered sides up. Close toaster and cook for 3-4 minutes or until pastry is crisp and golden. Serve hot or cold with whipped cream or ice cream.

Apricot and Sweet Potato Pie

Serves 4

1 quantity Shortcrust or Puff Pastry (see pages 52 or 53) or 1 packet frozen pastry
melted butter for brushing
125 g sweet potatoes, cooked and mashed
1 cup apricots, fresh or canned and drained
2 tablespoons cream
2 tablespoons brown sugar, or to taste
½ teaspoon salt
½ teaspoon ground cinnamon
¼ teaspoon nutmeg
1 egg yolk, lightly beaten
sour or fresh cream for serving

This is similar to Pumpkin Pie above. It can be made with either Shortcrust or Puff Pastry.
Roll pastry to thickness of 3 mm. Cut pastry to fit scallops and brush 1 side of each piece lightly with melted butter. Preheat Sandwich Toaster. Combine all ingredients, adjusting the amount of sugar to suit your taste. Lay a piece of pastry into each scallop and fill with mixture. Top with remaining pastry, buttered sides up. Close toaster and cook for 3-4 minutes or until crisp and golden. Serve hot or cold with cream.

Italian Turnovers

Serves 4

non-stick cooking spray
1 quantity Shortcrust Pastry (see page 53) or 1 packet frozen shortcrust pastry
½ cup grape jam
90 g walnuts, crushed
60 g cooking chocolate, grated
¼ teaspoon ground cinnamon
1 tablespoon rum or ½ teaspoon rum essence
fresh or sour cream for serving

Spray scallops with non-stick cooking spray or brush lightly with melted butter. Roll pastry to 3 mm thick and cut to fit scallops. Preheat Sandwich Toaster. Combine jam, nuts, chocolate, cinnamon and rum or rum essence. Lay pastry into scallops. Use a quarter of the filling for each turnover. Cover with remaining pastry. Close lid and cook for 3-4 minutes or until pastry is crisp and golden. Serve hot or cold with whipped fresh or sour cream.

Scots Bun

1 quantity Shortcrust Pastry (see
    page 53) or 1 packet frozen
    shortcrust pastry
melted butter for brushing
125 g seedless raisins
125 g currants
60 g walnuts, chopped
60 g sugar
60 g ground almonds
¼ teaspoon each ground allspice,
    ginger, cinnamon, black pepper
1-2 tablespoons brandy or whisky
    or milk
1 egg yolk

This rich Scottish cake is traditionally eaten on New Year's Eve, Hogmanay. The recipe adapts very well to the Electric Jaffle because when cold it can be sliced into fingers, although you can make it in a Sandwich Toaster as well.

Roll pastry to about 3-mm thickness. Cut into 10-cm squares for the Sandwich Toaster or 10 x 12 cm for the Electric Jaffle. Lightly butter 1 side of each piece of pastry. Combine the dried fruits, nuts and spices thoroughly in a mixing bowl. Add 1 tablespoon of brandy or milk and the egg yolk and mix the ingredients together until they are lightly bound. It may be necessary to add a little more liquid.

Preheat Sandwich Toaster. Lay 1 square of pastry into each scallop, buttered side down, and add enough of the filling to come level with the top of the scallops. Cover with remaining pastry, buttered sides up. Close lid and cook for 5-7 minutes or until pastry is crisp and golden. Serve cold.

Note: These keep very well in an airtight tin and improve with storage.

Baklava
(Pictured on page 48)

Syrup

3¼ cups water
3 cups sugar
juice of 1 large lemon
3 tablespoons orange flower water

Filling

200 g walnuts, coarsely ground
200 g almonds, coarsely ground
2 tablespoons sugar
2 teaspoons ground cinnamon
2 tablespoons butter, melted
1 x 375-g package filo pastry
½-¾ cup melted butter for
    brushing

These syrup-soaked pastries are easy to make and their flavour improves if they are left to thoroughly soak up the syrup until cold. Make the syrup first and chill it before pouring over the hot Baklava.

Syrup

Prepare the syrup by placing the water and sugar in a saucepan. Dissolve the sugar over a fairly low heat stirring constantly. When the sugar has dissolved completely add the lemon juice and bring the mixture to boil. Reduce the heat and simmer until the syrup thickens and is reduced to about 2½ cups. This will take 15-20 minutes. Stir in the orange flower water and simmer for 2 minutes more. Remove syrup from heat, pour into a jug and refrigerate. Use when very cold.

Note: If using the Snackmaker or Sandwich Toaster with cutter across centre, turn Baklava halfway through the cooking time. If using the Electric Jaffle lightly score the surface of the hot Baklava in diagonal strokes before pouring the syrup over.

Filling

Combine all the filling ingredients together thoroughly. Brush filo pastry sheets with melted butter using 10 buttered sheets for each layer. Preheat Sandwich Toaster. Cut pastry sheets to fit toaster scallops. Place 10-thickness layers, buttered sides down, into scallops and spoon enough filling onto pastry to bring it level with top of scallops. Cover with remaining layers of filo, buttered sides up. Close toaster and cook for 3-4 minutes or until crisp and golden brown. Pour cold syrup over hot pastries. Allow to cool before serving.

Spring rolls

Spring roll skins are now readily available, pre-prepared, from most supermarket freezer cabinets, gourmet delicatessens and Asian food stores. A wide variety of fillings may be used in the skins thus making spring rolls ideal to serve at parties, lunches, as a snack or an appetiser, especially if you have prepared Chinese food for the main course.

Brush 1 side of each spring roll skin with vegetable oil and lay the oiled sides together in a stack of pairs so that the top skin is an un-oiled one. Cover with a lightly dampened cloth while you are preparing the filling. This will prevent the skins from drying out too quickly.

Spring rolls may be cooked rolled, as you would a parcel, folding the ends in to enclose the filling, or by placing the filling in the centre of each skin and folding the 4 corners of the square into the centre to form an envelope.

Chicken Spring Rolls

Makes 8

8 spring roll skins
vegetable oil for brushing
125 g ham, minced or finely
   chopped
1 cup diced cooked chicken
6 water chestnuts, chopped
3 teaspoons soy sauce
1 egg yolk, lightly beaten
1-2 teaspoons fresh grated ginger

Brush 1 side of each spring roll skin with vegetable oil. Mix filling ingredients thoroughly together. Preheat Sandwich Toaster. Fill skins with chicken mixture as described above. Cook for 4-5 minutes. Serve with Chinese hot sauce or chilli sauce.
Variation: Duck Spring Rolls. Substitute 1 cup diced cooked duck for the chicken. Prepare and cook as above. Serve with Chinese plum sauce.

Scallop Spring Rolls

Makes 14-16

1 tablespoon vegetable oil
125 g scallops, trimmed and
   chopped
6 button mushrooms, finely
   chopped
1 small onion, finely chopped
½ teaspoon grated fresh ginger
salt to taste
1 cup bean sprouts, fresh or
   canned
1 teaspoon soy sauce
1 teaspoon dry sherry
14-16 spring roll skins
vegetable oil for brushing

Heat 1 tablespoon vegetable oil in pan or wok. Lightly fry scallops for half a minute, add mushrooms and onion and cook for 1 minute longer. Stir in ginger, mix well and sprinkle lightly with salt. Add bean sprouts, well drained if they are canned, soy sauce and sherry. Mix well. Brush 1 side of each spring roll skin with vegetable oil. Preheat Sandwich Toaster. Fill skins and fold as described above. Cook for 3-4 minutes or until crisp. Delicious served with Black Bean Sauce (see page 99).

Prawn Spring Rolls

Makes 8-10

8-10 spring roll skins
vegetable oil for brushing
250 g small cooked prawns
6 shallots (spring onions),
   cut into 5-mm rings
6 water chestnuts, chopped
2 teaspoons soy sauce
1 teaspoon cornflour
2 teaspoons brandy

Brush 1 side of each spring roll skin with vegetable oil, stack and cover with damp cloth while making filling. Mix prawns, shallots and water chestnuts together. Combine soy sauce, cornflour and brandy and mix through prawns. Preheat Sandwich Toaster. Fill spring roll skins and fold as described opposite. Cook for 4-5 minutes. Soy or chilli sauce can be served with them for dipping.

Pork and Mushroom Spring Rolls

Makes 12

125 g lean pork, minced
2 tablespoons vegetable oil
1 small onion, finely chopped
125 g mushrooms, chopped
6 water chestnuts, chopped
125 g ham, finely diced
½ cup bean sprouts, fresh or
   canned
1 teaspoon cornflour
2-3 teaspoons soy sauce
12 spring roll skins
vegetable oil for brushing

Cook minced pork in oil for 2-3 minutes until the colour changes. Stir while cooking to break up any lumps. Add onion and cook for further 2 minutes. Add mushrooms and cook for 1 minute longer. Combine pork mixture with water chestnuts, ham and bean sprouts (if using canned bean sprouts, drain well before adding to mixture). Mix cornflour with soy sauce and stir into mixture until well combined. Preheat Sandwich Toaster. Brush 1 side of each spring roll skin with vegetable oil. Fill skins with pork and mushroom mixture and fold as described opposite. Cook for 4-5 minutes. Serve hot with soy or chilli sauce.

Nut Date Spring Rolls

Makes 12-14

½ cup chopped walnuts
250 g dessert dates, pitted and
   chopped
grated rind 1 orange
½ teaspoon cornflour
½ teaspoon rose water, optional
1 tablespoon orange juice
12-14 spring roll skins
vegetable oil for brushing

Combine walnuts, dates and orange rind. Mix cornflour with rose water and orange juice and stir into fruit-nut mixture. Preheat Sandwich Toaster. Lightly brush 1 side of each spring roll skin with vegetable oil. Fill spring roll skins and cook for 3-4 minutes. Serve with whipped cream or lightly dusted with icing sugar.
Note: If using the Electric Jaffle or Sandwich Toaster with a cutter diagonally across the centre, place half a cup of mixture into the centre of spring roll skin and fold each corner to the centre, across the filling, to form an envelope. Cook for 4-5 minutes.

Pork and Crab Spring Rolls

(Pictured opposite)
Makes 8-12

250 g pork, finely minced
1 small onion, finely chopped
1 tablespoon vegetable oil
8-12 spring roll skins
vegetable oil for brushing
6 water chestnuts, chopped
1 x 220-g can crabmeat, drained
    and flaked
2-3 teaspoons soy sauce
1 x 55-g egg yolk, beaten

Lightly fry minced pork and onion in 1 tablespoon oil until pork changes colour. Stir pork as it is cooking to break up any lumps. Set aside. Brush 1 side of each spring roll skin with vegetable oil. Lay oiled skins together in a stack so that the top skin is an un-oiled surface. Cover with a slightly dampened cloth to prevent drying. Preheat Sandwich Toaster. Combine pork mixture with chopped water chestnuts, crabmeat and soy sauce. Add beaten egg yolk and mix well. Place a quarter cup of the mixture onto each skin, roll up as a parcel making sure that the filling is well enclosed inside each skin. Cook for 4-5 minutes. Serve hot with soy or chilli sauce.

Vegetable Spring Rolls

Makes 12-14

2 tablespoons vegetable oil
1 clove garlic, crushed
2 cm fresh ginger, grated
6 shallots (spring onions), cut into
    5-cm rings
1 cup finely sliced cabbage
2 canned bamboo shoots, drained
    and chopped
6 water chestnuts, chopped
1 tablespoon soy sauce
3-4 drops sesame oil, optional
salt to taste
½ cup bean sprouts, fresh or
    canned
1 tablespoon cornflour
1-2 eggs, lightly beaten
12-14 spring roll skins
vegetable oil for brushing

Heat oil in pan or wok and lightly fry garlic, ginger and shallots for 2 minutes, without browning. Add cabbage and fry for 2 minutes longer, stirring all the ingredients together. Add bamboo shoots and water chestnuts with soy sauce and sesame oil. Stir thoroughly and season with salt if necessary. Stir in bean sprouts (if using canned sprouts make sure they are well drained). Sprinkle mixture with cornflour and stir well. Remove pan from heat and use just enough egg to bind mixture loosely together. Cool. Lightly brush 1 side of each spring roll skin with vegetable oil. Preheat Sandwich Toaster. Fill skins as described on page 64, and cook for 4-5 minutes. Serve with chilli sauce if liked.

The versatile Snackmaker will cook Pork and Crab Spring Rolls (see above) perfectly. The attractive design was achieved by turning the rolls in the scallops during cooking time.

Doughs and batters

Scone and yeast doughs may be cooked successfully in a Sandwich Toaster, Snackmaker or Electric Jaffle. Scones may be made and cooked in minutes, whether you make your own or buy frozen scone dough or the convenient packet mixes. The same applies to yeast doughs, your own or frozen, so try the pizza recipes and spoil your family by preparing each person's favourite filling.

Pizzas

Make your own dough from the recipe overleaf or use frozen bread dough, then select a filling recipe. Even if you use the fillings in sandwiches, the end results will be delicious. Quantities in the following recipes for pizza fillings are enough to make 1 pizza but the amounts may be doubled or increased 4 or 6 times, depending on the number of people you wish to serve. Since it is so easy to vary the filling ingredients for the pizzas, each person may enjoy a different combination.

Roll the dough to a thickness of 1 cm. Frozen bread dough once thawed, may be treated in the same way. Cut the dough to fit the scallops. You may need to leave it a little larger to make room for the filling. Then brush 1 side of each piece with melted butter, fill with prepared ingredients, top with remaining pieces buttered sides up and cook for 5-6 minutes or until golden brown.

If you are using bread, butter the slices on 1 side and cook with the buttered sides against the scallops for 2 minutes.

An Electric Jaffle or Snackmaker is perfect to cook individual pizzas such as the Anchovy Pizza (see page 71). Each member of the family may choose his or her favourite taste combination.

Basic Pizza Dough

1 teaspoon sugar
10 g compressed yeast
⅔ cup warm water
2 cups plain flour
½ teaspoon salt
2 tablespoons oil

Dissolve sugar with the yeast in warm water. Sift flour and salt together into a large mixing bowl. Make a well in the centre and pour in the yeast mixture and the oil. Beat with your hand or use a mixer with dough hook, until a smooth dough forms. Turn dough onto a lightly floured board and knead for 3-4 minutes. Place dough into an oiled mixing bowl, cover with a towel and leave for approximately 2 hours in a warm place until dough has doubled in size. Punch dough down, knead lightly and roll out to a thickness of 1 cm. Cut into squares to fit scallops and use as directed in recipes.

Rich Pizza Dough

2 cups plain flour
½ teaspoon salt
15 g fresh yeast or 7-g sachet dried
   yeast
1 teaspoon sugar
⅓ cup warm milk
2 eggs, lightly beaten
60 g butter, melted

If using dried yeast in this recipe, first sprinkle the yeast onto the warm milk. When the yeast begins to ferment, it will start to bubble. Use in the same way as directed below.
Sift flour with salt into a mixing bowl. Cream the fresh yeast with the sugar (if using dried yeast see above). Mix the warm milk with the eggs and butter and add to the yeast mixture. Pour yeast mixture onto the flour and beat together using your hand or dough hook attachment of a mixer. Cover dough and leave in a warm place for approximately 30 minutes until dough has doubled in size. Punch dough down and knead lightly before rolling to a thickness of 1 cm. Cut into squares to fit scallops and use as directed.

Mushroom Pizza

Serves 1

Pizza Dough (see above) or 2
   slices bread
melted butter for brushing
2 teaspoons tomato paste
1-2 cocktail onions, chopped
4 canned button mushrooms,
   sliced
2 tablespoons grated cheese
4 green olives, stoned and halved
pinch dried oregano or basil,
   optional

Roll dough to thickness of 1 cm, cut to fit scallops and brush melted butter onto 1 side of each piece. If using bread, butter 1 side of each slice. Preheat Sandwich Toaster. Spread tomato paste on unbuttered sides of dough or bread. Lay dough or bread, buttered side down, into scallops, add remaining ingredients in given order. Top with bread or dough, buttered side up, and close lid. Cook dough for 5-6 minutes, bread for 2 minutes.

Anchovy Pizza
(Pictured on page 68)
Serves 1

Pizza Dough (see opposite) or 2
    slices bread
melted butter for brushing
2 teaspoons tomato paste
4 anchovy fillets
2 slices tomato
3 stuffed olives, chopped
2 tablespoons grated mozzarella
    cheese

Follow procedure for Mushroom Pizza opposite.

Cabanossi Pizza

Serves 1

Pizza Dough (see opposite) or 2
    slices bread
melted butter for brushing
2 teaspoons tomato paste
¼ cup finely sliced cabanossi
    sausage
2 teaspoons chopped gherkin
¼ cup grated sharp (tasty) cheese

Follow procedure for Mushroom Pizza opposite.

Pepperoni and Mushroom Pizza

Serves 1

Pizza Dough (see opposite) or 2
    slices bread
melted butter for brushing
2 teaspoons tomato paste
4 canned button mushrooms,
    drained and sliced
8 slices pepperoni sausage, cut in
    5-mm rings
2 teaspoons grated Parmesan
    cheese

Follow procedure for Mushroom Pizza opposite.

Salami Pizza

Serves 1

Pizza Dough (see opposite) or 2
    slices bread
melted butter for brushing
2 teaspoons tomato paste
1 tablespoon grated Parmesan
    cheese
4 slices Italian salami
3 black olives, stoned and chopped

Follow procedure for Mushroom Pizza opposite.

Ham and Artichoke Pizza

Serves 1

**Pizza Dough (see page 70) or 2
  slices bread**
melted butter for brushing
2 teaspoons tomato paste
2 slices prosciutto ham
**2 canned artichoke hearts, drained
  and thinly sliced**
**2 teaspoons grated Parmesan
  cheese**

Follow procedure for Mushroom Pizza (see page 70).

Ham and Pineapple Pizza

Serves 1

**Pizza Dough (see page 70) or 2
  slices bread**
melted butter for brushing
2 teaspoons tomato paste
2 cocktail onions, chopped
60 g ham, chopped
**2 tablespoons drained, crushed
  pineapple, fresh or canned**
**1 tablespoon grated sharp (tasty)
  cheese**

Follow procedure for Mushroom Pizza (see page 70).

Prawn and Asparagus Pizza

Serves 1

**Pizza Dough (see page 70) or 2
  slices bread**
melted butter for brushing
2 teaspoons tomato paste
**60 g prawns, cooked, peeled and
  cut into 2-cm lengths**
**1 tablespoon grated mozzarella
  cheese**
**1 tablespoon drained asparagus
  tips**

Follow procedure for Mushroom Pizza (see page 70).

Neopolitan Pizza

Serves 1

**Pizza Dough (see page 70) or 2
 slices bread
melted butter for brushing
2 teaspoons tomato paste
1 small tomato, finely sliced
¼ teaspoon dried marjoram
2 tablespoons grated mozzarella
 cheese**

Follow procedure for Mushroom Pizza (see page 70).

Little Pizza

Serves 1

**Pizza Dough (see page 70) or 2
 slices bread
melted butter for brushing
2 teaspoons tomato paste
2 thin slices bel paese or pastorella
 cheese
4 anchovies, chopped
¼ teaspoon dried marjoram**

*This version of the Italian pizzetta, miniature pizza, is
ideal for cooking in the Sandwich Toaster. Turn pizza
halfway through cooking time, to cut into small size.*
Roll dough to 1-cm thickness and cut to size. Brush 1 side
of each piece of dough or each slice of bread with melted
butter. Preheat Sandwich Toaster. Spread unbuttered
side of bread or dough with tomato paste and lay
buttered side down into scallop. Layer with cheese,
anchovies and marjoram. Cover with remaining bread or
dough, buttered side up. Lower lid and cook bread for 1
minute, turn sandwich and cook for 1 minute more. Cook
dough for 2-2½ minutes, turn and finish cooking.

Country Pizza

Serves 1

**¼ quantity Shortcrust Pastry (see
 page 53) or 2 slices bread
2 teaspoons cream cheese
30 g ham, chopped
1 tablespoon grated Parmesan
 cheese
1 small hard-boiled egg, chopped**

*This adaptation of the Italian Pizza Rustica is one of the
few which is also tasty when eaten cold. Shortcrust
Pastry is usually used for this pizza but bread can be
substituted.*
Preheat Sandwich Toaster. If using pastry roll to
thickness of 4 mm and cut to fit scallops. Butter 1 side of
bread or pastry, spread unbuttered side with cream
cheese and lay, buttered side down, into scallop. Add
chopped ham, Parmesan cheese and chopped egg.
Cover with remaining pastry or bread, buttered side up.
Close lid and cook pastry for 4-5 minutes, bread for 2
minutes.

Scones

Sandwich Toasters and Snackmakers are ideal to cook scones quickly. Serve them hot and buttered or cold with jam and whipped cream. What could be nicer with mid-morning coffee or afternoon tea!

Basic Scone Dough

Makes 10-12

2 cups self-raising flour
¼ teaspoon salt
60 g butter
1 cup milk
non-stick cooking spray

Sift flour and salt together. Rub butter lightly into the flour using the tips of your fingers. Add three-quarters of the milk to the flour, mixing the ingredients together quickly to form a soft dough. Add only enough of the remaining milk to soften the dough if it is too heavy. Turn dough onto a lightly floured board and knead lightly.

Preheat Sandwich Toaster and spray scallops with non-stick cooking spray. Roll dough to a thickness of 2 cm and cut into 2.5-cm squares or circles. Place a scone into each scallop of the Sandwich Toaster, close lid and cook for 5-7 minutes.

Note: If using the Electric Jaffle 2 scones can be cooked in each scallop.

Variations: Cheese Scones. Add half a cup of grated cheese to basic mixture before adding milk. Cook for 5-7 minutes.

Orange Scones. Using Basic Scone Dough, add 3 tablespoons sugar and 2 teaspoons of finely grated orange peel to dry ingredients. Mix to soft dough with approximately 1 cup orange juice instead of milk. Cook for 4-6 minutes. (These are pictured on page 77.)

Sultana Scones. Add 60 g sultanas to dry ingredients before mixing to a dough. Cook for 5-6 minutes.

Wholemeal Scones

Makes 6-8

1 cup plain flour
¾ cup plain wholemeal flour
½ teaspoon salt
½ teaspoon baking powder
1 teaspoon cream of tartar
non-stick cooking spray
2 tablespoons butter
½ cup buttermilk or whole milk

Sift dry ingredients into a mixing bowl and make a well in the centre. Set aside. Spray scallops with non-stick cooking spray or brush lightly with butter. Preheat Sandwich Toaster. Melt the butter and add the buttermilk. Heat until just lukewarm. Pour liquid into the dry ingredients and combine to form a soft dough.

Turn dough onto a lightly floured board, knead lightly until smooth. Roll to a thickness of 1 cm and cut into 9-x-4-cm rectangles. Cook in scallops with lid closed but unclamped for 4-5 minutes. Serve hot or cold with butter or savoury filling.

Variation: Wholemeal Cheese Scones. Add 60 g grated Parmesan cheese to dry ingredients before adding liquid. Cook as above.

Raised Scones

Makes 6-8

2 cups plain flour
½ teaspoon salt
½ teaspoon baking powder
1 teaspoon cream of tartar
non-stick cooking spray
30 g butter, melted
¾ cup light sour cream

Sift flour into mixing bowl with salt, baking powder and cream of tartar. Spray scallops with non-stick spray and preheat Sandwich Toaster. Make a well in the centre of the flour. Mix the melted butter with sour cream and pour into centre of dry ingredients. Mix together until a soft, but not sticky dough is formed. The mixing should be done as lightly and quickly as possible.
Turn dough onto a lightly floured board and knead until smooth. Roll dough to a thickness of 2 cm and cut into 2.5-cm squares or rounds. Place scones into scallops and close lid. Cook for 5-6 minutes. Serve hot and buttered or cold with jam and whipped cream.

Swedish Scones

Makes 10-12

non-stick cooking spray
⅓ cup sultanas
⅓ cup chopped nuts
½ teaspoon mixed spices
1 quantity Basic Scone Dough (see opposite)
strawberry jam

Preheat Sandwich Toaster and spray scallops with non-stick cooking spray. Mix sultanas, nuts and spices together. Roll scone dough thinly and cut into 18-cm squares. Spread jam thinly over the 10-cm centre of each square. Sprinkle with sultanas, nuts and spices mixture. Fold the 4 corners of the square to the centre forming a sealed envelope. Place each scone in Sandwich Toaster and cook for 4-6 minutes until golden brown. Serve hot or cold, spread lightly with butter.

Easter Cakes

Makes 6-8

1 cup fine semolina
¾ cup melted butter
½ cup boiling water
non-stick cooking spray
icing sugar for dusting

Filling

1 teaspoon orange essence
2 teaspoons rose water
½ cup caster sugar
1 cup crushed walnuts

These moulded dough cakes keep very well in an airtight tin. Traditionally eaten at Easter time, they have an unusual flavour which can be enjoyed all year round.
Place semolina into a bowl. Melt butter, without browning, remove from heat and pour boiling water onto the butter. Pour water mixture onto the semolina, stirring constantly until ingredients are well combined. Knead until dough is smooth. Cover bowl and leave to rest for as long as possible. The dough can be made the day before. Spray scallops with non-stick cooking spray, and preheat Sandwich Toaster. Roll dough thinly to 1-cm thickness and cut to fit scallops. Lay a slice of dough into each scallop, sprinkle dough generously with filling, cover with another piece of dough. Close toaster and cook for 5-7 minutes. Dust lightly with icing sugar while still hot.

Filling

Mix orange essence and rose water together, add sugar and walnuts and combine well. The filling will have a crumbly appearance.

Waffles

When making waffles, use butter or non-stick spray on the plates before preheating the Wafflemaker. Use a quarter cup of waffle batter on each plate and close the lid firmly onto the batter to ensure an even spread of the mixture. An unevenly coloured waffle indicates that either the batter contains too much liquid or more mixture should be used. Waffles freeze well and may be re-crisped for a few minutes in a hot oven. To freeze waffles, seal in airtight packages. Your Wafflemaker has many other uses. Try the Waffled Onion Bread on page 81. Serve it with soup or wrap it around sausages or frankfurters. Waffled sandwiches not only taste good but are very attractive. There is a list of suggested fillings for waffled sandwiches on page 43.

French Waffles
(Pictured opposite)
Makes 12

2 cups plain flour
¾ teaspoon baking powder
30 g sugar
125 g butter, melted
2 x 50-g eggs
½ teaspoon vanilla essence
vegetable oil for brushing

Sift flour and baking powder together into a mixing bowl with the sugar. Pour the melted butter onto the lightly beaten eggs, add the vanilla essence and beat until just combined. Make a well in the centre of the dry ingredients, pour in the egg mixture and beat gradually together until thoroughly combined. Allow batter to stand for 30 minutes before using.

Lightly oil the waffle plates and preheat Wafflemaker. Spoon or pour a quarter cup of batter onto each waffle plate, close lid firmly to spread batter and cook until golden. Serve sandwiched with your favourite filling.

Serving Suggestions

Strawberry Waffles

1 punnet strawberries, hulled and thinly sliced (reserve a few whole strawberries for decoration)
1-2 tablespoons caster sugar
whipped cream or ice cream, optional

Strawberry Waffles

Slice strawberries, sprinkle with sugar to taste and allow to soak until sugar has dissolved. To serve, drain strawberries, reserve juice. Place a large tablespoon of the strawberries onto a waffle, top with another waffle and serve with cream or ice cream, if liked. Spoon a little of the strawberry juice over the top of the waffles.

Chocolate Waffles

ice cream
Chocolate Sauce (see page 97)

Chocolate Waffles

Serve sandwiched with ice cream and topped with hot Chocolate Sauce.

Kiwi Fruit Waffles

3 Kiwi fruits (Chinese gooseberries), peeled and sliced
1-2 tablespoons caster sugar
whipped cream or ice cream

Kiwi Fruit Waffles

Peel and slice Kiwi fruits, sprinkle with sugar to taste and allow to soak until sugar has dissolved. Fill waffles and top with cream or ice cream.

Crisp and golden French Waffles (see above) are cooked quickly in a Wafflemaker. They may be filled with sliced strawberries or a fruit of your choice. Orange Scones are a variation of the recipe for Basic Scone Dough (see page 74).

Basic Waffle Batter

Makes 12

2¼ cups self-raising flour
¼ teaspoon salt
3 tablespoons sugar
3 eggs, separated
1½ cups milk
6 tablespoons butter or margarine,
  melted

Sift flour and salt into a large bowl. Stir in sugar. Make a well in the centre. Combine egg yolks, milk and butter and gradually stir into the flour. Beat well to form a smooth batter. Whisk egg whites until stiff and gently fold into the mixture. Allow to stand for 10 minutes.

Brush waffle plates with a little vegetable oil and preheat Waflemaker. Use a quarter cup of batter for each waffle and cook for 3-5 minutes or until evenly browned.

Note: There is a selection of fruit sauces suitable for topping waffles, (recipes for sauces start on page 97).

Variations: Coconut. Add half a cup of shredded or desiccated coconut to waffle batter before folding in egg whites.

Ham. Omit sugar and add half a cup of finely chopped ham to batter before adding egg whites.

Citrus. Add 3 teaspoons grated lemon or orange rind to batter before adding egg whites. Serve with lemon gelato or Sweet Lemon Butter (see page 101).

Spicy Ginger Waffles

Makes 12

½ teaspoon bicarbonate of soda
1½ cups plain flour
1½ teaspoons baking powder
¼ teaspoon salt
½ teaspoon ground cinnamon
½ teaspoon ground ginger
2 eggs, separated
½ cup molasses or black treacle
½ cup water
½ cup milk
125 g butter, melted
vegetable oil for brushing

Sift dry ingredients together into a large mixing bowl. Beat egg yolks until light in colour, add molasses or black treacle and beat until thickened and fluffy. Gradually add milk, beating well between each addition. Pour egg mixture into the dry ingredients and beat until a smooth batter is formed. Add the melted butter and beat again until well combined. Whisk the egg whites until stiff and gently fold into the batter. Allow to stand for 15 minutes before using. Preheat Wafflemaker, brushing top and bottom plates with vegetable oil, butter or margarine. Pour a quarter cup of batter onto each waffle plate, close lid firmly to spread batter and cook for 4-5 minutes or until crisp and evenly brown. Serve hot with ice cream and Ginger Sauce (see page 98).

Note: Molasses or black treacle gives a better flavour but if unavailable golden syrup can be substituted.

Variation: Add 1 tablespoon finely chopped preserved ginger to the batter before adding egg whites.

Main dishes may also be prepared using a Snackmaker, Sandwich Toaster or Electric Jaffle. The meat and vegetables in Lamb Shashlyk (see page 84) cook quickly since both sides touch the plates at the same time. Serve with Cucumber Salad, Tabbouleh and Baked Pilaf (recipes are on pages 90, 91 and 93).

Golden Waffles

Makes 12

1 cup self-raising flour
1 teaspoon sugar
¼ teaspoon salt
2 eggs
1 cup unthickened cream
1 tablespoon melted butter
vegetable oil for brushing

Sift flour, sugar and salt together, set aside. Separate the eggs. Beat egg yolks until light and fluffy, stir in cream. Add dry ingredients to egg mixture, stirring until well combined, add melted butter and mix lightly. Brush plates of Wafflemaker with oil, butter or non-stick cooking spray. Preheat Wafflemaker. Beat egg whites until stiff and fold gently into the mixture. Spoon a quarter cup of mixture into each plate, close lid firmly to spread batter evenly and cook for 3-4 minutes or until crisp and golden. Serve with maple syrup and ice cream or your favourite topping.

Mrs Lorraine Fransdonk, 10 Silverton Drive, Ferntree Gully Vic. 3156.

Individual Bombe Alaskas

Serves 6

2 egg whites
pinch salt
⅓ cup caster sugar
6 waffles, pre-made with any of the waffle batters
6 scoops ice cream
¼ cup brandy, optional
2 tablespoons toasted slivered almonds
6 glacé cherries, optional

Beat egg whites and salt until stiff. Add sugar, 1 tablespoon at a time, beating well after each addition. Preheat grill.
Place a scoop of very cold ice cream on the centre of each waffle. Spread meringue mixture over each ice cream portion, making sure that ice cream is completely covered with meringue. Form meringue into peaks, and place waffles under the hot grill for a short time until peaks are golden. Watch carefully so that they do not become too dark. Heat brandy in a small saucepan, pour a little over each Bombe Alaska and carefully ignite. Sprinkle each Bombe with slivered nuts and cherries. Serve immediately.

Beer Waffles

Makes 12-14

3½ cups self-raising flour
¼ teaspoon salt
1 tablespoon sugar
2 x 60-g eggs, separated
370 ml beer
½ cup vegetable oil
¼ cup milk
2 tablespoons lemon juice
rind of 1 lemon, finely grated
vegetable oil for brushing

Sift flour, salt and sugar into a large mixing bowl. Make a well in the centre. Whisk together the egg yolks, beer, oil, milk and lemon juice. Stir in the lemon rind. Pour mixture into dry ingredients and stir until just combined. Beat until a smooth batter is formed. Whisk egg whites until stiff and fold gently into batter. Brush plates with vegetable oil or melted butter and preheat the Wafflemaker. Use a quarter cup of batter for each waffle and cook until golden for 3-5 minutes.

Banana Oatmeal Waffles

Makes 16

1 large banana, mashed
2 teaspoons lemon juice
1½ cups self-raising flour
½ teaspoon nutmeg
½ teaspoon salt
¾ cup rolled oats
2 eggs, separated
1 cup sugar
¾ cup milk
½ cup water
125 g butter, melted
vegetable oil for brushing

The texture of these waffles is slightly softer than most and they taste good when served hot with a little butter. Unlike most waffles they can be eaten cold and their taste is similar to American cookies.

Mix mashed banana with the lemon juice and set aside. Sift flour with nutmeg and salt into a large bowl and mix the rolled oats thoroughly into the flour. Beat egg yolks with the sugar until thickened. Add banana and beat until well mixed. Gradually add the milk and water, beating until the batter is smooth. Add the batter to the dry ingredients with the melted butter and beat until well mixed. Whisk the egg whites until stiff and fold into the batter. Allow the waffle mixture to stand for 10-15 minutes. Brush plates with oil or melted butter and preheat Wafflemaker. Pour a quarter cup of mixture onto hot waffle plates and cook for approximately 5-6 minutes.
Note: These waffles will freeze well or can be stored in the refrigerator and reheated.

Waffled Onion Bread

Makes 8-10

45 g butter
90 g onions, finely chopped
⅓ cup lukewarm water
½ teaspoon salt
1½ cups plain flour

This savoury flatbread is an excellent accompaniment to soups or use it in place of buns for hot dogs with a difference.

Melt 15 g of the butter in a frying-pan and gently fry the onions until softened but not browned, approximately 3-4 minutes. Remove the onions from the pan and cool. Melt the remaining butter in the pan and pour the resulting onion flavoured butter into a mixing bowl. Add the lukewarm water, cooled onions, salt and three-quarters of the flour to the butter and beat the ingredients together, using a spoon. Add only enough of the remaining flour to the mixture to make a dough that will not stick to your fingers. Knead the dough lightly in the bowl and divide it into 8 or 10 pieces. Using a lightly floured rolling pin roll each piece of dough thinly and trim to 10-cm squares. Re-knead trimmings until all the dough is rolled. Preheat Wafflemaker. The flatbreads should be cooked on an unoiled surface but if they appear to stick too much, spray waffle plates with a little non-stick cooking spray. Lay dough onto waffle plates, close and cook for 1½-2 minutes. The breads should have the mottled appearance of Lebanese bread instead of browning evenly. Cool on a rack and continue cooking until all the dough is used.
Note: The flatbreads freeze well; cool and seal them in airtight packages. To use frozen flatbreads reheat in a hot oven for 3-4 minutes.
Variation: Waffled Celery Flatbread. Substitute 90 g finely chopped celery for the onions.

Main courses

Steaks, hamburgers (homemade or frozen), meat patties and kebabs may all be cooked perfectly in a Sandwich Toaster, Snackmaker or an Electric Jaffle. The cooking time is short as both sides are cooked at once and the results are delicious.

Carpetbag Steak

Serves 1

1 eye fillet steak, 2 - 2.5 cm thick
non-stick cooking spray
3 fresh oysters, shelled
salt and freshly ground black
    pepper

Use Electric Jaffle for best results.
Using a very sharp knife, cut a pocket into the centre of steak, without cutting completely through the meat. Season lightly inside the pocket with salt and pepper to taste. Insert oysters into pocket, secure opening with cocktail sticks. Spray scallops of Electric Jaffle with non-stick cooking spray or brush lightly with butter. Cook steak according to taste: rare — 1½ minutes; medium — 2 minutes. Serve with Creamed Spinach (see page 93) or a crisp salad or vegetable of choice.
Note: Cooking times for steaks are shortened by using the Electric Jaffle as they are cooked on both sides at once.

Pepper Steak

Serves 1

1 eye fillet steak, cut 2 - 2.5 cm thick
1 teaspoon poivre vert, green
    peppercorns or whole black
    peppercorns, coarsely ground
salt to taste
non-stick cooking spray

Suitable for Electric Jaffle.
Using a very sharp knife, cut a small pocket in steak, making sure not to cut right through the meat. If using green peppercorns, mash them lightly with a fork before spreading inside the pocket. Season lightly with salt and secure with cocktail sticks. Crack black peppercorns or grind coarsely before inserting into pocket. Preheat Electric Jaffle and spray with non-stick cooking spray or brush lightly with butter. Cook for times given for Carpetbag Steak above. Serve with vegetables of choice or salad.

Fancy Frankfurters

Serves 4-6 as part of a meal
12-24 as appetisers

500 g frankfurter sausages, choose
   the extra long ones or tiny
   cocktail frankfurters
90 g samsoe or Edam cheese
1 large dill pickle
2 tablespoons crushed pineapple,
   drained if canned

Cut long frankfurters to fit scallops of Sandwich Toaster. Make a lengthways slit in each frankfurter being careful not to cut right through. Cut cheese and dill pickle into strips 5 mm thick and long enough to slip into the frankfurter pocket. Fill some of the frankfurters with cheese, some with dill pickle and some with drained pineapple. Preheat Sandwich Toaster, but do not oil the scallops. Secure filling into frankfurter with short pieces of cocktail sticks and cook for 2-3 minutes. Serve with Tomato Sauce (see page 99) or a commercial one and a Potato Salad (see page 91).
Note: Lay frankfurters straight into scallops of Snackmaker and Electric Jaffle and parallel to the cutter in the Sandwich Toaster.
Variation: Any favourite filling can be used. Wrap a short piece of bacon round the frankfurter before cooking.

Salmon and Potato Patties

Serves 2-4

1 x 220-g can salmon, drained and
   flaked
¾ cup mashed potatoes
1 small onion, grated
2 teaspoons lemon juice
1 tablespoon finely chopped
   parsley
1 egg yolk
salt and pepper to taste
non-stick cooking spray

Combine all ingredients together and shape into patties. Spray scallops with non-stick cooking spray and heat Sandwich Toaster. Cook patties for 5-6 minutes. Serve with fresh green vegetable of choice.
Note: Quantities to use in Breville appliances are:
Snackmaker and Snack 'n' Sandwich Toaster, generous quarter cup of mixture per scallop;
Electric Jaffle, generous third cup of mixture per scallop.
Variation: Tuna Onion Patties. Substitute 1 x 185-g can tuna and onion for salmon and omit grated onion.

Minced Meat and Mushroom Patties

Serves 4

185 g cooked meat, minced
1 onion, minced or finely chopped
185 g button mushrooms, chopped
2-3 teaspoons mushroom sauce,
   optional
2-3 teaspoons Worcestershire
   sauce
salt and pepper to taste
2 egg yolks, lightly beaten
non-stick cooking spray or oil for
   brushing
2-3 tablespoons flour or
   commercial crumbs

Almost any cooked meat, beef, lamb, pork or mutton can be used for these patties.
Combine all ingredients, except flour or crumbs, using enough of the beaten egg to bind the mixture together. Preheat Sandwich Toaster and spray scallops with non-stick cooking spray or brush with oil. Use a quarter cup of the mixture at a time and shape it roughly to fit scallop. Coat each patty lightly with flour or crumbs and place into scallops. Close toaster and cook for 4-5 minutes until patties are well browned. Serve hot or cold with vegetables or salad.

Kebabs
and shashlyks

Cooking kebabs or shashlyks in a Sandwich Toaster, Snackmaker or Electric Jaffle is very easy. Both sides are cooked at the same time, but you may have to turn them once. Basically the meat used is marinated and then threaded with other bits and pieces onto skewers. The variety of meats used and the simplicity of cooking kebabs this way allows a wide range of flavours to be combined, each of which is quite different. So whether you are cooking for 1 or many, an interesting dinner may be produced with minimal effort and expense.

Use the bamboo skewers which are readily available at most supermarkets and Asian supply shops. Remove about 2.5 cm from the end of each skewer then cut them in half. Allow 2 per serve, and as they cook so quickly you will be able to keep 1 batch hot while another is cooking.

Lamb Shashlyk

(Pictured on page 78)
Serves 4

Marinade

1 medium onion, minced or grated
2 teaspoons lemon juice
2 teaspoons olive or vegetable oil
½ teaspoon salt
¼ teaspoon freshly ground black
pepper

8 bamboo skewers, cut to scallop
length
500 g lean boneless lamb, cut into
2.5 - 3-cm cubes
melted butter for brushing or non-
stick cooking spray
8 small onions, quartered
1 red capsicum, cut into 2.5-cm
cubes
1 green capsicum, cut into 2.5-cm
cubes

Mix together grated onion, lemon juice, oil and seasoning. Add the meat and leave at room temperature for 2-3 hours, turning the meat occasionally in the marinade.

Brush scallops of Sandwich Toaster lightly with melted butter or use non-stick cooking spray and preheat. Thread marinated lamb onto skewers alternately with the quartered onions, red and green capsicums. Lay skewers into scallops, close lid, but do not clamp. Cook, making a half turn if necessary halfway through the cooking time, 5-7 minutes. Cooking for 5 minutes will produce lamb that is just cooked through but very juicy in the centre. If you prefer lamb very well cooked continue for the longer period. Serve hot with Cucumber Salad, Tabbouleh (mint and parsley salad) and Baked Pilaf (recipes on pages 90, 91 and 93).

Mutton Kebabs with Almonds

Serves 4

juice of 2 lemons
1 small onion, grated

**250 g lean leg mutton, cut into 2.5-
    cm cubes**
**vegetable oil for brushing or non-
    stick cooking spray**
4-6 bamboo skewers
salt and pepper to taste
1 cup light sour cream
60 g almonds, slivered and toasted

Mix lemon juice with the grated onion and turn mutton cubes in this mixture until thoroughly coated. Allow meat to marinate for 2 hours, turning occasionally.
Brush scallops with vegetable oil or use non-stick cooking spray. Preheat Sandwich Toaster or Electric Jaffle. Thread mutton onto skewers and season well with salt and pepper. Place kebabs into scallops and cook without clamping for 6-7 minutes, turning skewers a half turn if necessary. Serve on a bed of rice. Drizzle sour cream over the kebabs and sprinkle with almonds.
Note: Lamb may be substituted if mutton is not available. Serve with Baked Pilaf (see page 93).

Chicken Kebabs

Serves 4

Marinade

2 tablespoons white wine
1 tablespoon olive or vegetable oil
¼ teaspoon ground cinnamon
1 small onion, grated
½ teaspoon salt
freshly ground black pepper

2 whole chicken fillets, cubed
**1 green capsicum, seeded and cut
    into 2-cm squares**
4-6 bamboo skewers
30 g butter, melted

Combine marinade ingredients thoroughly and pour over the cubed chicken. Marinate the chicken for 1-1½ hours, turning the meat occasionally.
Drain chicken, reserving the marinade. Thread alternate pieces of marinated chicken and capsicum squares onto the skewers. Preheat Sandwich Toaster or Electric Jaffle. Pour marinade into a small saucepan and bring slowly to simmering point. Allow sauce to simmer.
Brush skewered chicken with melted butter, lay skewers into the toaster and cook with lid closed but unclamped for 3-4 minutes. Serve hot with rice or vegetables of choice, pouring a little of the sauce over each kebab.

Chicken Liver Brochettes

Serves 4

Marinade

1 small onion, grated
1 tablespoon medium dry sherry
1 clove garlic, crushed
½ teaspoon salt
1 bay leaf
1 tablespoon olive oil

250 g chicken livers, trimmed
90 g button mushrooms, halved
4-6 bamboo skewers
melted butter for brushing
3 tablespoons cream

Combine marinade ingredients and pour over the trimmed chicken livers. Marinate livers for 1-1½ hours, turning occasionally. Remove chicken livers from marinade and set aside. Quickly dip the mushrooms in the marinade and thread mushrooms and chicken livers alternatively onto the skewers. Pour remaining marinade into a small saucepan, discarding the bay leaf.
Brush scallops with melted butter and preheat Sandwich Toaster. Lay skewers into scallops and close toaster. Cook without clamping for 2-3 minutes. Bring the marinade rapidly to the boil. When boiling remove from heat and stir in the cream. Adjust seasoning and serve the Brochettes lightly coated with the sauce.
Variation: Substitute lamb kidneys for the chicken.

Cakes

with a difference

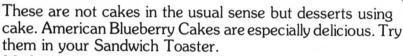

These are not cakes in the usual sense but desserts using cake. American Blueberry Cakes are especially delicious. Try them in your Sandwich Toaster.

Madeira cake, whether you make it yourself or buy a commercially produced one, has endless possibilities. Here are only a few suggestions but you could experiment with other mouth-watering combinations of fillings.

Apple Cakes

Serves 6-12

1 x 450-g slab stale Madeira cake
melted butter for brushing
3 Granny Smith apples, peeled,
    cored and finely sliced
2 teaspoons lemon juice
½ teaspoon mixed spices
1 teaspoon butter
1 tablespoon brown sugar or to
    taste
whipped cream for serving

Place sliced apples in a saucepan with the lemon juice. Simmer slowly together until apples are beginning to become transparent. Add mixed spices, butter and enough brown sugar to suit your own taste. Simmer gently until the apples are tender but not mushy.
Meanwhile preheat Sandwich Toaster. Cut Madeira cake into 5-mm slices. Trim cake to size. You may have to butt 2 slices together to fit the scallops. Brush 1 side of cake with butter. Lay cake, buttered sides down, into toaster. Spoon enough of the apple mixture into each scallop to bring it level with the top. Cover with remaining cake slices, buttered sides up, and cook for 1 minute. Serve hot or cold, with cream or ice cream if liked.

American Blueberry Cakes

Serves 4-8

1 x 450-g slab stale Madeira cake
melted butter for brushing
1 x 425-g can blueberries, drained
1 x 300-g carton heavy sour cream

Preheat Sandwich Toaster. Cut Madeira cake into 5-mm slices and brush 1 side with melted butter. Lay cake, buttered sides down, into scallops (you may need to butt 1 or 2 pieces together to line each scallop). Spoon enough of the blueberries onto the cake-lined scallops to come level with the scallop tops, cover with remaining cake, buttered sides up. Close toaster and cook for 1-1½ minutes. Serve hot or cold with sour cream.
Variations: Rhubarb Cakes. Replace blueberries with 1 x 450-g can rhubarb, drained, or use 1½ cups cooked fresh rhubarb.
Chocolate and Mandarin Cakes. Drain canned mandarins, fill cake-lined scallops with mandarin segments and sprinkle with chocolate vermicelli.

Cake Pudding

Serves 4

**4 x 2-cm thick slices fruit or sponge
cake
non-stick cooking spray
100 ml orange juice, fresh or any
other
whipped cream or Vanilla Sauce
(see page 98), for serving**

*Leftover fruit cake or stale sponge cake makes a
delicious dessert cooked this way.*
Trim cake slices to fit scallops. It does not matter if more
than 1 piece is used to fill each scallop, just butt them
together carefully and they will mould into 1. Preheat
Sandwich Toaster and spray scallops with non-stick
spray. Dip cake slices into orange juice and lay into
toaster scallops. Close toaster and cook for 1-1½
minutes. Serve hot with cream or Vanilla Sauce.
Note: If you intend to serve these cakes with the Vanilla
Sauce make it before the cakes are cooked.

Sponge Alaska

Serves 1

**2 x 1-cm slices Madeira or sponge
cake
melted butter for brushing
1 x 1-cm slice very cold ice cream,
cut to fit scallop**

Cook this just before serving.
Preheat Sandwich Toaster. Brush 1 side of each cake
slice with melted butter and lay a piece of cake, buttered
side down, into a scallop. Top with ice cream and cover
with remaining cake slice, buttered side up. Close toaster
and cook for 1 minute. Serve immediately.

Hazelnut Cream Fingers

(Pictured on page 96)
Serves 4-8

**16 Savoiardi (sponge finger)
biscuits
90 g butter, softened
30 g icing sugar, sifted
60 g ground hazelnuts (hazelnut
meal)**

*This makes an attractive dessert when cooked in a
Snackmaker but you can also cook the Fingers side by
side in the Electric Jaffle.*
Trim biscuits to scallop length. The trimmings can be
used in trifles or as cake crumbs for coatings. Cream
butter with icing sugar and hazelnuts until smooth and
creamy. Preheat Sandwich Toaster.
Spread a generous layer of hazelnut mixture between
pairs of biscuits and lightly brush the outsides of the
biscuits with the remaining mixture. Place filled biscuits
into scallops, close toaster and cook for 1 minute. Serve
cold with an Apricot or Rasberry Sauce, (see pages 97
and 98).
Variation: Lemon Cream Fingers. Make 1 quantity of
Sweet Lemon Butter (see page 101) and use to fill and
coat sponge fingers. Serve cold with whipped cream.

Accompaniments

Soups

Soup is a great beginning to a meal. When served with a toasted sandwich or savoury roll of a complementary flavour, soup is ideal for lunch or a late supper, especially on a cold night.

Carrot Soup

(Pictured on page 50)
Serves 4-6

500 g carrots, cut into 1-cm slices
1 large onion, chopped
30 g butter
1 stalk celery, cut into 1-cm lengths
1 clove garlic, crushed
4 cups chicken stock, or use cubes
salt and pepper to taste
½ cup cream
1 teaspoon finely chopped parsley
or mint

Fry carrots and onion in butter for 5-6 minutes. Add the celery and garlic and cook for 3-4 minutes longer. Add stock and season to taste with salt and pepper. Bring to the boil, then reduce heat and simmer carrots until tender, approximately 20 minutes. Using a slotted spoon, remove vegetables from the soup, and purée them in the Kitchen Wizz, a blender or push them through a sieve. Stir the purée back into the stock, bring to the boil and remove from heat. Stir in the cream, adjust seasoning and garnish with parsley or mint.

Mushroom Soup

Serves 4-6

250 g mushrooms, chopped
90 g butter
1 small clove garlic, crushed
1½ tablespoons flour
4 cups chicken stock, or use cubes
3 or 4 drops mushroom sauce,
optional
½ cup cream
2 teaspoons finely chopped parsley
salt and pepper to taste

Wipe mushrooms, do not peel. Trim off coarse ends of stalks. Melt butter in a saucepan and gently sauté the mushrooms until tender. Add crushed garlic and cook for 1 minute. Using a slotted spoon, remove mushrooms from the pan and set aside. Stir flour into pan juices, stirring well. Cook for 1 minute. Add 1 cup of stock to the pan, heat, and stirring constantly, cook the sauce until thickened. Add 1 more cup of stock and repeat. Remove sauce from the heat.

Purée mushrooms in Kitchen Wizz or blender or put through a sieve. Add a cup of the remaining stock to the mushroom purée and mushroom sauce to taste. Combine mushroom purée and sauce, stirring together until smooth. The soup should not be too thick so add only enough of the remaining stock to bring the soup to the consistency you prefer. Bring soup just to the boil, remove from the heat and stir in cream. Add chopped parsley and season to taste with salt and pepper. Serve hot with Waffled Onion Bread (see page 81) or any of the Savoury Rolls, (recipes begin on page 44).

Onion Soup

Serves 4-6

30 g butter
4 medium onions, finely sliced
1 tablespoon brown sugar
3 cups beef stock, use cubes
1-2 tablespoons brandy
salt and freshly ground black
    pepper

Melt butter in pan. Add finely sliced onions and cook slowly until onions are lightly browned. Sprinkle with sugar and cook for a further 4-5 minutes until sugar has melted and onion mixture is glazed. Add beef stock, bring quickly to the boil then reduce heat and simmer for 25-30 minutes. Add brandy and season to taste with salt and plenty of freshly ground black pepper. Serve very hot with savoury Cheese and Beer Rolls (see page 51).

Lettuce Soup

Serves 4-6

1 large lettuce, washed and
    shredded
2 cups chicken stock, or use cubes
30 g butter or margarine
3 tablespoons flour
½-1 cup milk
salt and pepper to taste
pinch nutmeg
½ cup cream, optional

The flavour of this soup is similar to asparagus. Make it with the outside leaves of lettuce or use a whole one.
Place shredded lettuce and chicken stock into a pan and cook gently for 20-30 minutes. Drain lettuce, reserving stock. Purée lettuce in Kitchen Wizz or blender or push through a sieve. Set aside.
Melt butter or margarine in a pan, stir in flour and cook gently for 1 minute. Add half a cup of milk to roux and when milk is hot beat into flour mixture. Add half a cup of reserved stock and when hot beat again. Continue with remaining stock until a smooth sauce is formed. Stir in puréed lettuce and season to taste with salt, pepper and nutmeg. Add remaining milk if soup is too thick; it should be thick enough to just coat the back of a spoon. Stir cream into soup just before serving. Serve hot or chilled with Asparagus Rolls (see page 51).
Note: If serving Lettuce Soup chilled, check the seasoning as cold food sometimes needs a little more.

Lentil Soup

Serves 4-6

3 cups lentils
1 small onion, quartered
3 cloves
1 bay leaf
2 rashers bacon, chopped
3 onions, chopped
15 g butter
4-5 cups beef stock, use cubes
salt and pepper to taste

Soak lentils overnight with quartered onion, cloves and bay leaf. Use enough water to cover the lentils. Drain lentils, reserving the soaking liquid. Discard quartered onion, cloves and bay leaf. Gently sauté bacon for 1 minute until the fat begins to run. Add chopped onions and butter and cook for 2-3 minutes longer. Set aside. Place drained lentils in a saucepan, add bacon and onion mixture, including any flavoured oil left in the pan. Increase the reserved soaking liquid to 5 cups, using water flavoured with beef stock cubes. Bring lentils to the boil, then reduce temperature and simmer until lentils are tender. Purée lentils in Kitchen Wizz or blender or push them through a sieve. Season to taste with salt and pepper. Serve hot with Garlic Rolls (see page 44) or any of the Savoury Rolls (recipes begin on page 44).

Salads

The right salad can complement a crisply toasted sandwich or pie and complete a tasty and nutritious snack. Some of these salads also make delicious fillings for toasted sandwiches. Try the Mushroom or Waldorf Salads in milk bread or puff pastry. Serve with another salad or a freshly cooked vegetable. The variations are simply endless.

Bean Sprout Salad

Serves 4-6

125 g fresh bean sprouts
1 lettuce, broken into serving pieces
1 cucumber, peeled and thinly sliced
2 stalks celery, cut into 2-cm pieces
2 tablespoons slivered almonds

Dressing

2 tablespoons olive or vegetable oil
2 teaspoons white vinegar
½ teaspoon soy sauce
½ teaspoon sugar
¼ teaspoon mustard
1 small clove garlic, crushed

Wash and dry bean sprouts and lettuce and mix in a bowl with cucumber slices and celery. Mix all the salad dressing ingredients together and just before serving pour over the salad. Toss well together and sprinkle with almonds.
Note: This salad complements Spring Rolls well (recipes begin on page 64).

Cucumber Salad
(Pictured on page 78)
Serves 4

¾ cup natural yoghurt
1 clove garlic, crushed
2 teaspoons finely chopped mint, or 1 teaspoon dried mint
salt and white pepper to taste
2 cucumbers, unpeeled and thinly sliced
mint leaves for garnish

This is a fresh and cooling salad which can be made in minutes.
Mix yoghurt with garlic and mint. Season to taste with salt and pepper. Cool in refrigerator until ready to serve salad.
Run the tines of a fork the length of each cucumber, pressing sufficiently to score the skin. Continue until the skin of each cucumber is striped. Trim the ends and slice the cucumbers very finely into rings. When ready to serve combine yoghurt with cucumbers and garnish with mint leaves.

Mushroom Salad

Serves 4

1 tablespoon white or wine vinegar
¼ teaspoon each salt and pepper
¼ teaspoon mustard powder
1 small clove garlic, crushed
¼ cup olive oil
1 tablespoon sour cream or
   2 teaspoons fresh cream mixed
   with
   2 teaspoons plain yoghurt
125 g button mushrooms, thinly
   sliced
125 g gruyère cheese, finely diced
125 g ham, finely diced

Mix vinegar with salt, pepper and mustard. Add garlic, oil and sour cream, or cream and yoghurt and mix thoroughly. Combine mushrooms, cheese and ham in a bowl and pour dressing over. Toss together lightly and chill before serving.
Note: Mushroom Salad also makes a good sandwich or pastry filling.

Potato Salad

Serves 4

500 g potatoes
salt and pepper to taste
1 tablespoon oil, preferably olive
1 clove garlic, peeled and left whole
½ cup white wine
3 shallots (spring onions), chopped
1 tablespoon finely chopped
   parsley
1 tablespoon capers
½ cup mayonnaise
1 hard-boiled egg, optional
1 small green capsicum, chopped
2 rashers bacon, crisply fried

Boil the potatoes with skins on until just tender. While still warm peel and cut into chunks. Season with salt and pepper and set aside. Heat oil in a small saucepan with garlic until hot but not boiling. Discard garlic. Pour wine over the potatoes, stir gently and sprinkle over the shallots, oil, parsley and capers. Stir in enough mayonnaise to bind the ingredients lightly together. Arrange sliced hard-boiled egg, chopped capsicum and crumbled bacon pieces on top. Chill and serve.

Tabbouleh
Mint and Parsley Salad
(Pictured on page 78)
Serves 4

1 cup fine burghul (cracked wheat)
1 cup finely chopped shallots
   (spring onions)
salt and pepper to taste
½ cup finely chopped mint
1½ cups finely chopped parsley or
   coriander
1 large tomato, chopped
¾ cup olive or vegetable oil
¾-1 cup lemon juice

Place burghul into a bowl, cover with water and leave for 1 hour to soften. Drain well and squeeze out any excess water. Mix burghul with the shallots, squeezing them together with your hands to extract some of the onion juice. Season with salt and pepper. Add the mint, parsley or coriander and combine thoroughly. Add tomato, oil and lemon juice, toss the ingredients together. Adjust the seasoning, adding a little more lemon juice if necessary. The salad should have sharp overtones.

Tomato Anchovy Salad

Serves 4

2 large or 4 small tomatoes, thinly
   sliced
4 anchovy fillets, chopped
8 black olives, stoned and roughly
   chopped
2 tablespoons white wine vinegar
freshly ground black pepper

Combine tomatoes, anchovies and olives in a bowl. Add vinegar and toss lightly. Season with pepper to taste. Chill before serving.

Waldorf Salad

Serves 4

1 cup diced cooked chicken
1 small red apple, unpeeled, cored
   and diced
1 small green apple, unpeeled,
   cored and diced
juice of ½ lemon
2 stalks celery, cut into 5-mm rings
30 g walnut halves, broken rather
   than chopped
½ cup mayonnaise
1 small or ½ large lettuce

Place chicken into a bowl. Sprinkle the chopped apples with the lemon juice, to prevent discolouration and add them to the chicken. Add celery and walnut pieces to the rest of the salad in the bowl and toss all together with the mayonnaise. Serve chilled on a bed of lettuce.
Note: Waldorf Salad also makes an excellent sandwich filling; shred the lettuce and mix in with the other ingredients.

Vegetables

Like salads, vegetables complete a meal and add valuable
nutrients to the diet as well as important roughage. Recipes
overleaf may be cooked in sandwich-toasting appliances.

Green Beans Almandine
(Pictured on page 95)
Serves 4

500 g green beans, sliced
½ teaspoon salt
1 small clove garlic, optional
30 g butter or margarine
60 g almonds, blanched and
**   slivered**
salt and pepper to taste

Cook beans in boiling salted water until just tender.
Drain. Crush garlic and cook gently in the butter for 2-3
minutes without browning the garlic. Add slivered
almonds and cook over a gentle heat until the almonds
are lightly tinged with brown. Add cooked beans to
almond mixture and toss until beans are hot and well
mixed with the almonds. Adjust seasoning.

Lemony Brussels Sprouts
Serves 4

500 g Brussels sprouts
½ teaspoon salt
30 g butter, melted
juice of ½-1 lemon
pepper to taste

Trim any discoloured outer leaves and stalks off sprouts.
Cut a small cross in the stalks at the base. Either steam
the sprouts with a sprinkling of salt or boil them in very
little water until just tender. They should remain in
perfect shape and be crisp. Drain and toss in melted
butter, add lemon juice and adjust seasoning.

Creamed Spinach
Serves 4

1 bunch spinach (silver beet)
60 g butter
salt to taste
4-5 tablespoons cream

Trim coarse stalks from spinach and wash thoroughly.
Place wet spinach into a large saucepan with the butter.
There is no need to add any more water. Cook over a
gentle heat until spinach is just cooked. Drain and purée
in Kitchen Wizz or blender or push through a sieve.
Season to taste with salt and add the cream.

Baked Pilaf
(Pictured on page 78)
Serves 4

1 cup long grain rice
2 cups hot stock, or use cubes

Preheat oven to 180°C (350°F). Place rice in a 1.5-litre
casserole. Heat stock or water and stock cubes until hot
but not quite boiling. Pour over the rice, cover casserole
and cook for 45 minutes.
Note: Use chicken stock with chicken, lamb and mutton
dishes. Beef or fish stock if appropriate.

Parsnip Patties

Serves 4-6

1 kg parsnips, peeled and sliced
½ teaspoon salt
⅓ cup flour
1 x 60-g egg
½ teaspoon nutmeg
2 tablespoons chopped parsley,
    optional
salt and freshly ground black
    pepper

Place sliced parsnips in a saucepan, cover with cold water, add salt and bring to the boil. Simmer until tender. Drain thoroughly and mash or purée in Kitchen Wizz or blender. Add flour to puréed parsnips and mix well. Bind with the egg and mix in nutmeg and parsley. Season to taste with salt and freshly ground black pepper. Spray scallops of Sandwich Toaster with non-stick cooking spray and preheat. Use about a third cup of mixture for each patty and cook 5-6 minutes.

Potato Patties
(Pictured opposite)
Serves 4

non-stick cooking spray
1½ cups mashed potato, firmly
    packed
1 egg yolk
1 teaspoon butter
salt and pepper to taste

Preheat Sandwich Toaster and spray each scallop with non-stick cooking spray. Combine all the ingredients and divide into scallop moulds. Close lid and cook for 5-6 minutes. Serve hot with steaks and salad.
Variations: Add any of the following to the basic mixture:
1 tablespoon prepared mustard and half a cup grated Cheddar cheese;
1 tablespoon finely chopped parsley;
2 rashers of finely chopped cooked bacon;
1 tablespoon chopped chives and 1 tablespoon sour cream.

Jansson's Temptation

Serves 4

3 medium-sized potatoes
non-stick cooking spray
1 small tin anchovies
1 small onion, minced
2 tablespoons cream
1 egg yolk
pepper to taste

This is a famous old Scandinavian dish, good enough to eat alone or to serve with grills and fish dishes.
Boil the potatoes in their skins until just cooked. Peel, slice thinly and set aside. Spray scallops with non-stick cooking spray and preheat Sandwich Toaster. Drain and chop the anchovies, reserving the oil. Mix the anchovies with the onion, cream and egg yolk. Place a layer of potatoes into the scallops, spread a teaspoon of anchovy mixture over the potatoes. Add another layer of potato and another layer of anchovies. Top with a last potato layer, sprinkle lightly with pepper and drizzle a little anchovy oil over each Temptation. Close lid firmly to compress the filling and cook for 3-3½ minutes.

Potato Patties (see above) provide an ideal way to use leftover mashed potato. They are an unusual accompaniment to Pepper Steak or Carpetbag Steak (see page 82). Top with Herb Butter (see page 100) and serve with Green Beans Almandine (see page 93), mushrooms and a crisp salad.

𝓢auces
and other accompaniments

Both sweet and savoury sauces have been included here. Some would be used as a 'topping' rather than a sauce. The fruit purées may be used as fillings as well as toppings for pies or waffles.

Apricot Sauce
(Pictured opposite)
Serves 4

1 cup apricot jam
3 teaspoons water
2 tablespoons whisky or brandy

It is worth making a larger quantity of Apricot Sauce since it stores well in the refrigerator and the freezer. Sieve the jam over a small saucepan or put through Kitchen Wizz or blender until thoroughly puréed and smooth. Add the water to the jam and cook over a gentle heat for about 5 minutes until slightly thickened. Remove from heat and stir in the whisky. Use with fruit pies or sandwiches.

Chocolate Sauce

1 tablespoon cornflour
1 tablespoon cocoa
30 g sugar, or to taste
¾ cup water
¼ teaspoon vanilla essence
¼ cup cream

Mix cornflour, cocoa and sugar in a small saucepan with 1 tablespoon of the water until smooth. Add remaining water and cook over a moderate heat until sauce thickens. Add vanilla essence and simmer for 2 minutes, stirring constantly. Remove sauce from heat, cool for 3-4 minutes and add the cream, mixing until sauce is smooth and shiny. Serve hot.
Variation: Chocolate Orange Sauce. Omit vanilla essence and use half cup of orange juice with a quarter cup of water and the grated rind of half an orange.

Fiesta Sauce

Serves 6

1 tablespoon arrowroot
1 cup water
⅓ cup orange juice concentrate (carton or frozen), use undiluted
¼ cup sugar
1 cup dried mixed fruit
2 tablespoons chopped almonds
1 tablespoon brandy

Blend arrowroot with a little of the water in a saucepan. Add remaining water and orange concentrate, sugar, mixed fruit, almonds and brandy. Bring to the boil, stirring constantly. Continue cooking until sauce is clear and has thickened. Reduce heat and simmer for 2 minutes. Serve hot on waffles, with ice cream if liked.

An attractive dessert, Hazelnut Cream Fingers (see page 87) are made from sponge finger biscuits and served with Apricot Sauce (see above).

Ginger Sauce

Serves 6

1 tablespoon arrowroot
1¼ cups water
1 tablespoon lemon juice
¼ cup sugar
1 teaspoon ground ginger
1½ tablespoons brandy
3-4 pieces preserved ginger, finely
 chopped (optional but nice)

Mix arrowroot with a little of the water until smooth. Add remaining water and lemon juice and pour liquid into a saucepan. Mix the sugar and ground ginger together and stir into the saucepan. Cook the sauce over a gentle heat, stirring constantly until the mixture boils. Continue to stir while the sauce simmers for a further 2 minutes. The sauce should be clear and not too thick. Add brandy and preserved ginger. Serve with waffles, pancakes and rhubarb desserts.

Raspberry Sauce

Serves 4

185 g frozen raspberries, thawed
1-2 tablespoons caster sugar
1½ teaspoons Kirsch
1 teaspoon arrowroot

This sauce has a thicker consistency and it is suitable to use as a filling as well as a topping for fruit pies and sandwiches.
Sieve raspberries over a small saucepan to remove pips. Add 1 tablespoon of the sugar, plus Kirsch and arrowroot and cook over a gentle heat until the sugar has dissolved and the sauce is clear and thickened. Add remaining sugar if necessary. Serve hot or chilled.

Vanilla Sauce

Serves 4

60 g caster sugar
1 tablespoon cornflour
pinch of salt
2 egg yolks
¾ cup cream
¾ cup milk
1 teaspoon vanilla essence

Mix sugar, cornflour and salt in a saucepan. Beat the egg yolks, lightly, with the cream and set aside. Use 2 tablespoons of the milk to mix cornflour and sugar to a smooth paste. Add the remaining milk and the egg and cream mixture to the pan. Cook over a gentle heat, stirring or whisking constantly until sauce is thick (3-4 minutes). Beat in vanilla essence and serve hot or cold.

Tutti Frutti Ice Cream

Serves 6-8

½ cup chopped raisins
⅓ cup chopped glacé cherries
½ cup marsala wine
1 cup cream, stiffly whipped
1 cup crushed macaroon biscuits
3 cups ice cream, softened

This is a delicious way to enhance the flavour of commercially produced ice cream and make it a special treat. Delicious served with waffles or use in Sponge Alaska (see page 87).
Place chopped raisins and cherries into a bowl, add marsala and stir until fruit is coated. Set aside and allow to soak for 1 hour. Fold whipped cream into the marinated fruit mixture, then add the crushed macaroons. Stir fruit mixture into softened ice cream and spoon mixture into a shallow tray. Freeze rapidly.

Cinnamon Sugar

3 tablespoons ground cinnamon
3 tablespoons caster sugar

This combination adds flavour to fresh and dried fruit dishes.
Place ingredients into a paper bag, shake together until well mixed and store in an airtight jar.

Black Bean Sauce

1 tablespoon salted black beans, rinsed and well mashed
2 tablespoons dry sherry
1 tablespoon water
2 tablespoons soy sauce
1 teaspoon sugar

Place all ingredients in Kitchen Wizz or blender and mix until rich and smooth. Store in an airtight jar in the refrigerator and use as desired. This is very good with fish and seafood dishes.

Herb Sauce

Serves 4

2 shallots (spring onions), finely chopped
1 teaspoon finely chopped parsley
¼ teaspoon dried tarragon
¼ teaspoon dried chervil
¼ teaspoon dried thyme
15 g butter
1 teaspoon flour
¼ cup milk
¼ cup cream
salt and pepper to taste
½ teaspoon French mustard
1 egg yolk, beaten with 1 tablespoon milk
1 teaspoon lemon juice

Cook the shallots and herbs gently in the butter for 5-6 minutes. Stir the flour into the saucepan and cook for 1 minute. Add the milk, stirring into the roux. When the milk is absorbed add cream and simmer gently, stirring, until the sauce is smooth and thickened. It must not boil. Season to taste with salt and pepper. Mix the mustard with the egg yolk and milk. Lightly beat into the sauce stirring constantly until thickened. The sauce must still not be allowed to boil. Adjust seasoning and just before serving add the lemon juice.

Tartare Sauce

½ cup mayonnaise
1 teaspoon chopped capers
1 teaspoon chopped gherkins
1 teaspoon fresh mixed herbs or ½ teaspoon dried mixed herbs
juice of ½ lemon
salt and pepper to taste

Combine all ingredients.
This can be served with most fish dishes as well as cold chicken and meats.

Tomato Sauce

250 ml tomato juice
2 teaspoons sugar
2 teaspoons Worcestershire sauce
1 tablespoon Dijon mustard

Mix all ingredients together until well blended. Simmer in a small saucepan for 10-15 minutes. Serve hot or cold.

Flavoured butters

The addition of flavouring to butter or margarine will make your toasted sandwiches or rolls even more tasty. The butters keep well in the refrigerator or freezer although unsalted butter will store for longer in a deep freeze than salted butter. The quantities given will yield 125 g of mixture.

Anchovy Butter

125 g butter, softened
1-2 teaspoons anchovy paste
1 teaspoon lemon juice

Beat butter with anchovy paste until well blended. Add lemon juice and beat until well combined.
Note: Use in rolls and sandwiches to be served as an hors d'oeuvre or with soups.

Garlic Butter

125 g butter, softened
2 large cloves garlic, crushed
salt and pepper to taste

Melt half the butter over a gentle heat. Add the crushed garlic and simmer gently for a few minutes without letting the garlic brown. Strain, cool and beat strained butter with remaining butter, season if necessary and use as desired.
Note: This is the quickest and easiest way to make garlic bread.
Variation: Instead of melting some of the butter with the garlic first, crush the garlic and beat into the softened butter, season and use. This method is best for use in the sandwiches or rolls as the garlic in the butter does not darken.

Herb Butter
(Pictured on page 95)

125 g butter, softened
1 teaspoon finely chopped parsley
1 teaspoon finely chopped chives
½ teaspoon freshly chopped
    rosemary or ¼ teaspoon dried
    rosemary
salt and pepper to taste

Combine all ingredients until completely blended. Cover and store in refrigerator until ready to use.

Lemon Butter

125 g butter, softened
3-4 teaspoons lemon juice
1 teaspoon finely grated lemon rind
2-3 drops tabasco sauce or
    sprinkling cayenne pepper
salt to taste

Beat butter with lemon juice, add lemon rind and tabasco or cayenne pepper and continue to beat until ingredients are well blended. Season to taste and use as desired.
Note: This is very suitable for fish and some vegetable fillings. The butter can also be rolled in foil, chilled and cut into medallions to serve with grilled fish.

Parsley Butter

125 g butter, softened
2-3 teaspoons finely chopped
   parsley
2 teaspoons lemon juice

Beat the butter until creamy. Beat in parsley and lemon juice and use as desired.
Note: This is particularly good with fish and cheese fillings.

Brandy Butter
Hard Sauce

60 g butter
⅓ cup icing sugar, sifted
1 tablespoon brandy

Cream the butter and beat in the icing sugar until light and fluffy. Beat brandy into the mixture and use as desired.
Note: This is delicious rolled into a sausage shape in foil, chilled and when cold sliced into medallions and served with Christmas pudding and mince pies.
Variation: Rum Butter. Replace brandy with 3 teaspoons rum and 1 teaspoon orange juice. This is particularly good with bananas.

Cinnamon Butter

90 g butter, softened
1 cup icing sugar
1 teaspoon ground cinnamon

Beat butter until creamy. Sift icing sugar with cinnamon and beat into butter until light and fluffy. Chill and use with fruit.
Note: This butter is particularly good with apple, rhubarb and banana fillings.
Variations: Replace cinnamon with equal amount of ground nutmeg or mixed spices.

Sweet Lemon Butter

90 g butter, softened
1 cup icing sugar, sifted
juice of 1-1½ lemons

Beat butter until creamy, add icing sugar and blend well. Beat in as much of the lemon juice as can be absorbed by the butter mixture. The butter should be really lemony. Use with sweet fruit fillings, cream cheese and peanut butter.

Index

Sandwich Toasters, Snackmakers and so on are handy appliances to use since you can produce a snack or a meal in minutes. For your convenience, the index has been cross-referenced so that if you have some eggs, tinned foods or leftover meat, for example, simply look up that particular item to find all the recipes which include it as a main ingredient. In addition recipes in each section for various types of sandwiches, quiches, rolls, waffles, pastries and so on are listed.